THE BIBLICAL NEW MOON

A Beginners Guide for Celebrating

A  Book ©

Kisha Gallagher

This booklet is a BEKY Book publication:
Books Encouraging the Kingdom of Yeshua.
www.bekybooks.com

ISBN-13: 9780996183956

DEDICATION

To Curtis, for making it all possible.
I love you to the moon and back.

CONTENTS

Glossary   7

Introduction   11

1   The Mysterious Moon   13
2   The Moon Proclaims the Gospel   21
3   Rosh Chodesh (The New Moon)   29
4   How to Celebrate Rosh Chodesh   47
5   The Hebrew Months and Their Themes   53
        Nisan/Aviv
        Iyar
        Sivan
        Tammuz
        Av
        Elul
        Tishrei
        Cheshvan
        Kislev
        Tevet
        Shevat
        Adar
        Adar II
6   Blessings and Poems for the New Moon   89
        Shehechiyanu (Blessing for Special Occasions)
        Birkat HaChodesh (Blessing the New Month)
        The Molad (Time Annoucement for New Month)
        Kiddush Levanah (Sanctification of the Moon)
        Simple Blessing for the New Month
        Poetry for the New Moon
            The Moon Walks by Sarah S. Walters
            Luny Tunes by Deborah Flanagan

Further Reading   97

References   99

About the Author   101

GLOSSARY

Adonai – my Lord.

Brit Chadashah – the New or Renewed Covenant, usually called the New Testament.

Chodesh (chodeshim, pl.) – the Hebrew word for month(s). Since all Hebrew months begin on the new moon, this word indicates both month and new moon. See also Strong's Hebrew definition of the numbers H2320 and H2318.

Counting the Omer – an omer is a measure equating to the tenth part of ephah. The Torah commands Israel to count seven weeks or forty-nine days beginning from the day on which the Omer, a sacrifice containing an omer-measure of barley, was offered in the Temple in Jerusalem, up until the day before an offering of wheat was brought to the Temple on Shavuot or Pentecost. (Leviticus 23:15-22)

Ecliptic – one of the imaginary coordinate lines that astronomers and navigators use in mapping the sky. The ecliptic plane is the path that the sun appears to take through the sky as a result of the earth's rotation. Most objects in the solar system, including the planets and the constellations, orbit near this plane and in the same direction around the sun as the earth. Thus, the ecliptic is also the starting point for the celestial coordinate system used by astronomers to pinpoint the location of every star, nebula, and galaxy.

Elohim – the Hebrew common noun for God or gods.

Gematria – Hebrew doesn't have a separate set of symbols for numbers. Instead, each letter and combination of letters also represent numerals. Thus, every word, phrase, and sentence can also be understood as a number. Gematria is the calculation of these alphanumerical occurrences. Rabbis and scholars use them to gain Biblical insight in the relationship between various words and ideas.

Gregorian calendar – the current western calendar. Pope Gregory XII introduced this calendar in 1582 as a reformation of the Julian calendar. Julius Caesar implemented the Julian calendar in 46 BCE. The emperor's system miscalculated the length of the solar year by eleven minutes, which eventually caused the seasons to fall out of sync with the calendar. Pope Gregory XII sought to correct this error in order to keep Easter in the spring of the year. For more information see: https://www.britannica.com/topic/Gregorian-calendar and https://www.britannica.com/science/Julian-calendar#ref177882

Haftarah – selections from the Prophets (in the Tanakh or Old Testament) that are read after the weekly Torah portion in the synagogue.

Hillel II – president of the Sanhedrin in 320-385 CE. He is attributed with creating the current fixed Jewish calendar.

Julian Calendar – see entry for Gregorian calendar.

Megillah (megillot, pl.) – Literally a scroll, but usually refers to the five scrolls of Esther, Song of Songs, Lamentations, Ecclesiastes, and Ruth, which are read at the festivals of Purim, Unleavened Bread, Tish B'Av, Tabernacles, and Pentecost respectively.

Sanhedrin – the ancient Jewish court system of judges. This body was organized as a fulfillment of Exodus 18:21-22: "Furthermore, you shall select out of all the people able men who fear God, men of truth, those who hate dishonest gain; and you shall place these over them as leaders of thousands, of hundreds, of fifties and of tens. Let them judge the people at all times; and let it be that every major dispute they will bring to you, but every minor dispute they themselves will judge. So it will be easier for you, and they will bear the burden with you." (NASB) The Sanhedrin existed until about 425 CE when it was disbanded due to Roman and Christian persecution.

Tisha B'Av – the 9th of Av, a traditional fast day commemorating the destruction of the first and second Temples. Learn more in Chapter Five under the heading "Chodesh Av."

Tanakh – the complete Torah, Prophets, and Writings. Also called the Old Testament.

Torah – often translated as law, teaching, or instructions. The Torah refers to the five Books of Moses or the Pentateuch. Depending on context, it can also refer to the entire Old Testament or Tanakh. You can learn more about the Torah in the BEKY Book entitled: *What is the Torah?*, by Dr. Hollisa Alewine.

Shamash – Hebrew word for servant.

Siddur – a Jewish prayer book.

Tu B'Av – the 15th of Av, a traditional day of rejoicing and love. Learn more in Chapter Five under the heading Chodesh Av.

Tu B'Shevat – the 15th day of the Jewish month of Shevat. This is a Jewish traditional holiday also known as the New Year for Trees. Tu B'Shevat is observed for the purpose of calculating the age of trees for tithing. In Leviticus 19:23-25, fruit from trees may not be eaten during the first three years; the fourth year's fruit is holy to Adonai, and after that, the fruit is edible. Though this date is not in the Torah, having a specific time marked in the year to track a tree's fruit and age ensures that Leviticus 19 is followed.

Yeshua – Hebrew name of Jesus.

YHWH – the tetragrammaton or the four-letter name of God in Hebrew (yohd, hey, vav, hey). The LORD, Yahweh, Yehovah, or Jehovah. This author chose the four English letters YHWH to represent the Divine Name.

INTRODUCTION

When the moon hits your eye
Like a big pizza pie,
That's amore! [1]

The primary purpose of this BEKY Book is to give the reader a better understanding of how to celebrate the new moon. It is NOT a book about proper crescent moon sightings or calendar calculations. Instead, this book conveys the excitement and the profound joy that comes from meeting the Creator at one of His often forgotten festivals. Additionally, this book will help you to prepare and organize a delightful setting to celebrate each new month and dedicate it to the Creator.

Time is something that we all cherish. In the hustle and bustle of our busy lives, it is difficult to carve out those extra hours and minutes that are necessary to strengthen our spiritual lives. Family and work duties can gobble up our clocks and calendars if we are not diligent to plan our days with purpose. Of course, there is nothing wrong with having a family or a career, but we cannot let these obligations come before our relationship with the King of the Universe. This is one reason that the LORD (YHWH) [2] gave us His divine appointments. He knew that we would need His hallmarks in time to keep our lives balanced.

One who is returning to the LORD's Sabbaths, feast days, and Torah, knows all too well that preparation is the key to moving into His cycles without stress. When we meet with the King, we don't want any hindrances that will steal our zeal or joy.

God's calendar gives believers an opportunity to meet with Him every week on Sabbath, every month

1. Martin, Dean. *That's Amore the Best of Dean Martin.* Capitol, 1996. MP3.

2. The tetragrammaton or the four-letter name of God in Hebrew (yohd, hey, vav, hey). The LORD, Yahweh, Yehovah, or Jehovah. This author chose the four English letters YHWH to represent the Divine Name.

11

at the new moon, and at various times throughout the year on His feast days. The Creator of the universe is indeed concerned about how we spend our **time**. Families gather to fellowship, reminisce, and plan for the future. Families also celebrate life in all of its ups and downs and support one another through crisis and triumphs. From the very beginning, this has been the plan and purpose of the Creator as well. He beckons His children to meet with Him because they are His family, and He wants them to remember the past and to look forward to the future. In a word, He wants to BLESS us at His appointed times.

Realizing that the Creator of the Universe designed a calendar full of appointments and anniversaries just for His family is extraordinary. Like any parent, He desires that His children call often (pray) and visit when He asks (appointed times). These desires come from a place of profound love. Obviously, we can meet with Him at any time, any day, or any hour. He is always available to us. But there is something special about the gatherings that He has established. He has particular messages, blessings, and wisdom that He wishes to impart on His appointed days. Mankind is reminded of the Creator's vast *amore* (love) every time that the moon hits the eye.

1

THE MYSTERIOUS MOON

The moon has mesmerized mankind since the dawn of time. It has been deified by false religions and venerated in poetry, song, artwork, and literature. Being the closest celestial body to earth, it has captivated young and old astronomers alike. The moon has played a role in many ancient myths and was even a key player in the great Space Race of the twentieth century. Being the only heavenly body that we can see in detail with the naked eye, the moon's mystery is almost tangible. No generation, race, or creed has been untouched by the moon's silvery light.

The moon's changing phases have conjured some very speculative ideas in ancient and even modern societies. Many have suggested that the moon can produce mental illness, insanity, or even demonic possession. English words such as lunatic, lunacy, and moonstruck all originate with the assumption that the moon can trigger madness. Thus, it shouldn't be surprising to find that "sighting the new moon" is a point of controversy and strife even among those returning to the Torah [3]. Even reading about these debates can make one feel as if he is losing his mind!

Nevertheless, when we gaze up into the night sky, the

3. The Torah, often translated as law, teaching, or instructions refers to the five Books of Moses or the Pentateuch. Depending on context, it can also refer to the entire Old Testament or Tanakh. You can learn more about the Torah in the BEKY Book entitled: *What is the Torah?*, by Dr. Hollisa Alewine.

moon's majesty beckons us to question its purpose and function. Throughout the centuries, the moon's shimmering face has comforted sojourners and homesick travelers. No matter how far they travel away from home, the same moon gives a gentle glow in the darkness of night. In like fashion, curious little children are sure that this heavenly night-light follows them wherever they go. The moon is nothing if not mysterious.

What does the Bible have to say about the moon? Why is there an emphasis on new moon celebrations? These questions will be answered in meeting the following objectives, which are to determine:

- The purpose that the Creator assigns to the heavenly luminaries.
- The message that the moon speaks.
- The methods with which ancient Israel celebrated *Rosh Chodesh* (the new moon).
- The methods with which modern Judaism celebrates Rosh Chodesh.
- The ways in which followers of Jesus (Yeshua) can celebrate the new moon today.

The Purpose of Celestial Bodies

Before we rocket straight to the moon, it is necessary to consider the other luminaries. Adonai (the LORD) has a purpose and a function for all of the heavenly hosts. They are meant to provide the earth with physical **light**, but these natural bodies have a spiritual duty as well. In his explanation of the resurrection of the dead, the Apostle Paul explains that the natural heavenly bodies also have a spiritual purpose.

> There are also heavenly bodies and earthly bodies, but the glory of the heavenly is one, and the glory of the earthly is another. **There is one glory of the sun, and another glory of the moon, and another glory of the stars;**

for star differs from star in glory. So also is the resurrection of the dead. It is sown a perishable body, it is raised an imperishable body; it is sown in dishonor, it is raised in glory; it is sown in weakness, it is raised in power; it is sown a natural body, it is raised a spiritual body. **If there is a natural body, there is also a spiritual body.** So also it is written, "The first MAN, Adam, BECAME A LIVING SOUL." The last Adam became a life-giving spirit. However, **the spiritual is not first, but the natural; then the spiritual.** The first man is from the earth, earthy; the second man is from heaven. As is the earthy, so also are those who are earthy; and as is the heavenly, so also are those who are heavenly. Just as we have borne the image of the earthy, we will also bear the image of the heavenly. (1 Corinthians 15:40-49 NASB)

The natural things come first so that humans can recognize spiritual realities. The natural light of the sun, moon, and stars are meant to inform mankind of the truth of spiritual light. There is both natural light and spiritual light. One learns the former in order to perceive the latter. This requires us to think both literally and figuratively. Let's start at the beginning.

Then God said, "Let there be lights in the expanse of the heavens to separate the day from the night, and **let them be for signs and for seasons and for days and years**; and let them be for lights in the expanse of the heavens **to give light on the earth**"; and it was so. God made the two great lights, the greater light to govern the day, and **the lesser light**

to govern the night; He made the stars also. God placed them in the expanse of the heavens to give light on the earth, and to govern the day and the night, and **to separate the light from the darkness**; and God saw that it was good. There was evening and there was morning, a **fourth day**. (Gen. 1:14-19 NASB)

On day four of creation, Adonai explains the purpose or function of the sun, moon, and stars. They:

1. Separate the day from the night.
2. Are for signs, seasons, days, and years.
3. Give light to the earth.
4. Govern day and night.
5. Separate light from darkness.

These are the literal purposes of the luminaries. We don't have to stretch very far to understand our need for physical light. Living creatures and plants survive on earth because of natural light; this is elementary science. However, if this is true in the natural, could it be said that living creatures also require "spiritual" light in order to live? Reread the five points above, but this time, think figuratively. Could all five points also refer to spiritual light?

Heavenly Governors

The heavenly bodies were assigned a **governing** role in the creation. Their light and cycles track days, months, and years. The great luminaries govern earth's clocks and calendars. They are master timekeepers and servants of the Most High.

In verse fourteen above, it states that one of the governing actions of the luminaries is to serve as signs, seasons, days, and years. The days and years are pretty self-explanatory, so focus on the signs and seasons. The Hebrew word for signs is *oht*. It literally means a mark, signal, omen, or flag. The heavenly lights declare the glory of God, and they give signals or warnings of things to come. An *oht* or sign can remind of past events or forewarn of future ones (prophesy). The star that led the wise men to baby Yeshua is one example of an *oht* [4].

The Hebrew word for seasons in verse fourteen is *moedim*. A *moed* most often refers to the feast days or festival calendar of Adonai. The moedim are appointed times of gathering together with the assembly in worship and service [5]. These divine appointments with the Creator either remind of a past event or point us toward a future fulfillment [6]. Thus, the signs, seasons, days, and years are all linked to God's time clock or calendar. We may have understood our need for the physical light of the heavenly bodies, but have we forgotten our equally important need for their spiritual light? How can a calendar or time clock be spiritual?

Consider what calendars do. They **govern** lives by directing what we do with our **time**. Calendars dictate when we celebrate, when we rest, when we work, and when we gather together. They also mark important appointments and anniversaries. If the Creator felt that His calendar required the actual sun, moon, and stars to guard, protect, keep, and mark His special events, how much more should His people regard His calendar?

Our appointments with Adonai give spiritual light much in the same way that the sun, moon, and stars give natural light. They separate the light from the darkness. **If mankind ignores these appointments, he will have less light, less revelation.** The guardians of God's calendar speak to every creature on earth summoning us to come and meet with the Creator. King David said it this way:

4. Matthew 2

5. Leviticus 23 outlines the LORD's Sabbath and His seven Feasts.

6. Valerie Moody has written an excellent explanation of these celebrations in her book, *The Feasts of Adonai: Why Christians Should Look at the Biblical Feasts.*

17

> The heavens declare the glory of God; and the firmament shows His handiwork. **Day unto day utters speech, and night unto night reveals knowledge**. There is no speech nor language where their voice is not heard. (Psalm 19:1-3 NKJV)

The heavens have a voice and a message to proclaim. What have they been declaring to the world all this time? The Hebrew word for knowledge in the above verse is da'at [7]. This type of knowledge is an intimate knowing and carries with it the idea of sacrificial love [8]. It is the "bone of my bone and flesh of my flesh" that Adam experienced with Chavah (Eve) when she conceived and bore a son [9]. It is the loving knowledge that provoked Yeshua (Jesus) to lay down His life for His people. In both instances, the sacrificial love and knowledge of da'at brought forth **new life**.

Daily, the light of the sun overcomes the darkness of the night. Renewal, rebirth, growth, and change are displayed monthly in the moon phases. And the stars, particularly the primary constellations that fall in the same ecliptic as the sun, are believed by many to silently tell the entire Gospel story [10].

The heavens, the moedim (feasts), and the Gospel all communicate the same thing, for they all have the same Author. Their (spiritual) message and purpose is to proclaim the Gospel. It is a message of LIFE and LIGHT. The **moon** declares the good news and how to celebrate this loving message at Rosh Chodesh (new moon).

7. Strong's numbers H1847 and H3045

8. Da'at is one of the seven Spirits of God. (Isaiah 11:2) You can learn more about these seven in Dr. Hollisa Alewine's Creation Gospel series, beginning with Workbook One: http://www.thecreationgospel.com

9. Genesis 4:1

10. For example, see these titles: Mazzaroth, or the Constellations by Frances Rolleston, The Witness of the Stars by E. W. Bullinger, and The Gospel in the Stars by Joseph A. Seiss.

18

CHAPTER ONE REVIEW

1. Can you find some other examples of an *oht* (heavenly sign) in the Bible?

2. Look up the Hebrew word *moed* or *moedim* in a Hebrew concordance such Strong's. Read through some of the verses to see how it is translated. *Moed* is connected to the feasts, harvests, gathering, seasons, and even the people (assembly). Why do you think this is the case?

3. How do the sun, moon, and stars govern? What do they govern?

4. Do we serve these governors or do they serve us?

5. Most false worship involves the veneration of the sun, moon, and/or stars. Why do you suppose mankind has a problem with this? Is it possible that the enemy desires to pervert the true message of the heavenly hosts?

6. Read all of Psalm 19. What are the heavens silently proclaiming with their wordless speech?

7. Read Romans 10:14-18. Paul quotes Psalm 19 in this passage. To what message is he referring?

8. Have you ever considered that the heavenly luminaries, the Torah, the feasts of Adonai, and the gospels all proclaim the same message to us in various ways? What do you think this message is?

THE MOON PROCLAIMS THE GOSPEL

He made the moon for the seasons
(*moedim*); The sun knows the place
of its setting. (Psalm 104:19 NASB)

Rebirth

The moon is responsible for marking the timing of new months. Each new moon begins a new Hebrew month. The moon is even in our English word for month (**moon**th). This role is exclusive to the moon in the guardianship of the moedim (feasts). Months distinguish or mark out the time for seasons and festivals. While the sun and stars share in this responsibility, the moon beckons mankind to watch it a little more closely. According to the above Psalm, God made the moon **for the sake of the feasts** (*l'moedim*).

How does the moon serve Yeshua's disciples in the festival calendar? First, it physically makes believers aware of the timing of the months, which in turn informs of the dates of the moedim (feasts). Secondly, it exposes spiritual realities or light. The spiritual message of the moon is revealed in its cycle of waxing and waning and in its phases from darkness to light. Both of these services GIVE light to the earth.

The moon's constant phases remind us that even in our failings, when our light decreases, there is always hope for renewal. The moon also teaches about the reality of (spiritual) darkness and the need for the (spiritual) light of Messiah. Perhaps this is one reason that Yeshua revealed to Nicodemus the need to be born again at nighttime. The moon would have been visible in the evening sky as the two spoke about heavenly things. While it's possible that Nicodemus may have wanted to question the Master under the cover of darkness, Yeshua allowed their physical surroundings to teach spiritual truth: "*You must be born again* [11]."

Renewal

Let's consider some fascinating facts about the moon. The moon always shows the same side or face. From our perspective, the moon and sun look as if they are the same size. This is because the sun is about 400 times bigger than the moon, but it's also approximately 400 times further away, making these two very different celestial bodies appear similar in size. Moreover, the moon has no light of its own; its surface reflects the light from the sun back down to the earth.

This makes for some interesting metaphors. Like the moon, humans have more than one face, yet, we are designed to mirror only one image to the earth [12]. The Creator's bondservants are His reflection to a dark and dying world. Though we are much smaller in glory and majesty, we are often the only image of *Elohim* (God) that people see. In this way, we "appear" to be the same size as the sun (Son). We are His hands and feet that bring good tidings and comfort to the lost and hurting.

Similar comparisons can be made when considering the various moon phases. The regular arrival of the new moon and its growth to fullness, followed by its soon disappearance, has long been a visible symbol

11. John 3:7

12. For example, consider Jeff Benner of the Ancient Hebrew Research Center's explanation of "face": "The face reflects the many different moods, emotions, and thoughts of the person. The Hebrew word paniym (Strong's #6440) means "face," but is always written in the plural form (the "im" suffix identifies this word as plural), reflecting this idea of multiple faces of each person. This word can also mean "presence" or the "wholeness of being" of an individual." http://www. ancient-hebrew. org/language_ aaronic.html

of life, death, and rebirth. With every new moon, we see the necessity of being renewed (born again). This rhythmic clock sets a believer's calendar with each cycle marked as a new month (**moon**th).

This symbol becomes even more interesting when one considers that the Assembly of Adonai and the Body of Messiah are likened to a woman, daughter, sister, virgin, bride, and wife [13]. Like clockwork, the physical bodies of women go through *phases* each month. Similar to the moon, a woman's monthly cycle is directly linked to life, death, and rebirth. Each month a woman's womb prepares its "soil" for life and then sheds it (death) if no viable seed is planted — only to renew itself once again. This cycle repeats again and again. When a woman's body is in the shedding stage of menses, blood appears. When the moon gives a warning of judgment (death), it appears red. It's not a coincidence that this is a "blood moon".

Each appointed time or feast day of Adonai occurs during a particular moon phase. Each festival teaches an aspect of the Gospel or the Good News [14]. We will focus on the **new moon** lunar phase; however, take note of the entire moon cycle each month. According to David, the moon has a voice and utters speech. It is one of the heavenly witnesses.

> This is the message we have heard from Him and announce to you, that **God is Light**, and in Him there is no darkness at all. (1 John 1:5 NASB)

The moon has long been a metaphor for God's people in both Jewish and Christian teachings. Those that have taken the time to consider the course of the moon's cycles have not missed this luminous allegory. God is Light, and if we are His, we are the children of Light. But our light is not our own, we are a "lesser" light (like the moon) that can only reflect His brilliance and majesty.

13. For example: Isaiah 37:22; 54: 5-6; 62:5, Jeremiah 2:32; 18:13; 31:4, 21, Lamentations 2:13, Amos 5:2, John 3:29, 2 Corinthians 11:2, Revelation 19:7, etc. Also consider the allegory of the woman in the Song of Songs.

14. You can read more about the connections between the feasts, moon phases, and the new birth cycle on my blog series entitled *Moonbeams and the Moedim* Part I-IV at graceintorah.net

23

As one moves through the Creator's calendar each year, it becomes apparent that the moon continually reveals truth. For example, the festivals of Passover and Tabernacles are the first and last of the three pilgrimage (foot) feasts. They are like the bookends for Adonai's festivals. Since they both occur during the full moon, there is *more light* (both physically and spiritually).

Family, friends, and neighbors might conclude that you are **lunatic** for keeping "Old Testament" (Torah); but if they are curious at all, it will usually be during one of these **full moon festivals**. Because there is more natural light during these feasts, there is also more **spiritual light**! When this happens, embrace them into your festivities and reflect (like the moon) the love of our Messiah.

The Moon Walks

> If I beheld the sun when it shined,
> or **the moon walking in brightness**...
> (Job 31:26 KJV)

This author was a child when Michael Jackson made history by moonwalking on stage as he sang "Billie Jean" in 1983. His movement mesmerized my young eyes along with the rest of the world. Single steps blurred and flowed into one fluid motion, as he seemed to magically glide backwards across the stage. His dance moves appeared so otherworldly that these steps are forever ingrained in our culture as the "**moonwalk.**"

Interestingly, Job declares that the moon indeed **walks** (*halakh*) [15]. As it marches across the stage of the heavens, are we receiving its message? Night after night it faithfully performs for the whole world. Monthly, its gravity pulls on the vast oceans creating high and low tides. The closer its orbit comes to the earth, the higher the tide. Are we watching? Can we hear its silent voice and see its dance?

15. H1980

24

Michael Jackson wore a shiny sequined glove as he moonwalked across the stage, captivating multitudes. I believe that God means for His children to sparkle with the rays of His moonbeams so that we too, attract the world [16]. We become the true **moonwalkers** when we reflect His glory. Along with the moon, the heavenly feast days choreograph our interpretive dance steps through life. This graceful ballet whispers the Good News to thirsty and hungry souls with each new cycle.

The world still imitates the moonwalk of the acclaimed "pop king", which should provoke disciples of Yeshua to wonder if our walk through this life is truly imitating the heavenly steps of our King, Yeshua.

> For you were formerly darkness, but now **you are Light in the Lord; walk as children of Light** (for the fruit of the Light consists in all goodness and righteousness and truth), **trying to learn what is pleasing to the Lord.** (Ephesians 5:8-10 NASB)

16. For more see my article, *Moonbeams and the Moedim Parts I-IV* at graceintorah.net

CHAPTER TWO REVIEW

Read John 3:1-21.

1. Where does Nicodemus say that Yeshua came from? What is Yeshua's response to Nicodemus' statement? (vs. 3)

2. Look up the phrase "born again" in a Greek dictionary such as Strong's. What did you notice about the Greek word *anothen*? Do you suspect that Yeshua and Nicodemus may have actually looked up when they discussed this?

3. In verse 10, Yeshua seems to chide Nicodemus. If being "born from above" was a radical new concept, why would Yeshua have spoken to him in this manner? Do you suppose that Yeshua's message could have been proclaimed from the beginning in both the Word and in Creation, and that Nicodemus was aware of this?

4. What other comparisons of physical and spiritual things did Yeshua use in this passage to help seekers to understand the Good News?

5. In what ways can believers be compared to the moon? Can you think of some ways that are not mentioned above?

6. If the moon only shows one face or side, what can we learn from this? What "face" should we be showing the world?

7. How does the moon symbolize life, death, and new birth?

8. Read John 3:16-26. What do you think John meant by "He must increase, but I must decrease" in verse 30? Does this imagery remind you of the moon's phases?

9. Light is seen with the eyes. Sometimes a believer's message isn't something that needs to be heard, but something that needs to be observed (like the new moon.) How do we "show" the world the Good News? (Matthew 5:16)

10. Compare Matthew 5:16, Ephesians 5:8-10, 1 John 2:5-6, and 2 John 1:6. How do these verses describe the "walk" of a true follower of the Messiah? Is this prefigured in the natural world through the path or "walk" of the moon?

ROSH CHODESH (THE NEW MOON)

Moon Clock

The current western Gregorian calendar is **solar**-based. The sun fixes the timing of the months and years. The moon is sorely absent from its accounting. On the other hand, the Hebrew calendar is lunar-solar based. Every month (and year) begins at the new moon, but the sun is consulted to keep the seasons in balance. Essentially, the current western calendar, as helpful as it may be, is not the design of the Creator.

So Biblically speaking, how do we know when a month begins? In Hebrew, the word for month literally means new moon:

Strong's H2320

חֹדֶשׁ chôdesh From H2318; the new moon; by implication a month: - month (-ly), new moon.

The nightly change of light reflected by the moon can be compared to a clock with hands. Every night a little more or a little less light is visible. It's as if a giant hand is ticking slowly around the clock or moon's face. When we see the new moon sliver, it is akin to the hour hand striking twelve to start a new cycle (month). This idea is embedded so deeply in the Hebrew language that it uses the same word to describe both a new moon and a month.

Chodesh (new moon/month) comes from the Hebrew root chadash meaning to renew, rebuild, or repair [17]. The new month is like the previous months restarted and repeated in the cycle of time. You might be familiar with this term in the transliterated name for the New Covenant/Testament, Brit Chadashah. Like the new moon or month, the New Covenant is a renewal of the Old Covenant [18]. Thus, at the renewal or rebirth of the moon, a new month begins.

According to modern science, the new moon occurs when the moon is completely dark or when it is reflecting no light at all. We call this an **astronomical new moon** or the **conjunction** of when the moon is perfectly between the sun and the earth. The biblical new moon occurs when the first sliver of light becomes visible just after this dark moon.

In Jewish history, two witnesses had to physically sight the first sliver of the waxing moon crescent and report it to the Sanhedrin (ruling body) before a new month could be declared. When the moon is still black, there is not yet an indication of renewal. Only when the first tiny visible sign of light returns can the moon be considered "renewed."

17. Strong's H2318 châ dash A primitive root; to be new; causatively to rebuild: - renew, repair.

18. Jeremiah 31:31-34; Hebrews 8:7-13. Notice that the fault of the first covenant was the people, not Adonai's commandments or promises.

New Moon in Scripture

Of all of the biblical holidays, the new moon is perhaps the most overlooked. Compared to the other feast days, the new moon is rarely mentioned in the Bible. In those few references, even less instruction is given. The Bible seems to leave this celebration in obscurity. However, when the new moon does make its appearance in the Scriptures, the context clearly alludes to this festival's great significance. It is almost as if the moon **phases** in and out of the biblical text just like it does in our night sky.

The moon's cycle of being concealed and then revealed is another indicator of spiritual truth. The first commandment that Adonai gave to the children of Israel just before He redeemed them from the bondage of Egypt was about the new moon.

> Now the LORD said to Moses and Aaron in the land of Egypt, "This month shall be the beginning of months for you; it is to be the first month of the year to you. (Exodus 12:1-2 NASB)

This verse says, "This **chodesh** shall be the head of the **chodeshim** for you, it is to be the first **chodesh** of the year to you." This statement and its following instructions were given just prior to the tenth plague on Egypt. The (new moon) month of Aviv or Nisan would serve as the New Year on God's moedim (feast) calendar. This month occurs in the spring around March/April on the Gregorian calendar.

In the first month of the Biblical calendar, Adonai's Passover is commemorated. Pesach (Passover) is so vital to our walk with God that He declares it the FIRST of our months. It commemorates rebirth after He redeems His own from the clutches of Egypt and Pharaoh (metaphorically, the world, sin, and death). Our spiritual darkness is pierced with His spiritual light.

Adonai concealed the growing nation of Israel in the darkness of the womb of Egypt. When the fullness of time arrived, His people were born (revealed) through the blood of the lamb on their doorposts and the waters of the Reed (Red) Sea. The new moon was the sign that the time had come, and it is still a set memorial on God's calendar. Later, the Messiah would mirror this activity just as He told Nicodemus.

The moon's message remains the same: "You must be born again."

New Moon in the Torah

The five Books of Moses (Torah) do not have much instruction about the new moon. The Book of Numbers gives us this little snippet:

> "Also in the day of your gladness and in your appointed feasts, and **on the first days of your months,** you shall blow the trumpets over your burnt offerings, and over the sacrifices of your peace offerings; and they shall be as a reminder of you before your God. I am the LORD your God." (Numbers 10:10 NASB)

The verse above indicates that trumpets were blown on the new moons. This serves as a reminder that the LORD is our God and we are His. Without a standing Temple or Levitical priesthood, no animal sacrifices can be rendered. We can, however, offer the calves of our lips (blessings and prayers) as Hosea declares [19].

The Torah also mentions the new moon in conjunction with the Feast of Trumpets, often called *Yom Teruah* or Rosh Hashanah. This is the fifth festival in the yearly cycle of the moedim, and it is the only feast that occurs on a new moon. While there is no **direct** mention in the Torah that regular new moons are Sabbath days, the *chodesh* of the seventh month clearly is.

19. Take with you words, and turn to the LORD: say unto him, Take away all iniquity, and receive us graciously: so will we render the calves of our lips. (Hosea 14:2 KJV)

> Again the LORD spoke to Moses, saying, "Speak to the sons of Israel, saying, 'In the seventh month **on the first of the month** you shall have a **rest**, a reminder by blowing of trumpets, **a holy convocation. 'You shall not**

do any laborious work, but you shall present an offering by fire to the LORD.'"(Leviticus 23:23-25 NASB)

New Moon in the Prophets and the Writings

King Saul and David kept the new moon as a two-day feast. (1 Sam. 20) Clouds and weather can affect the sighting of the new moon. This is one reason that the festival lasted for two days. Jewish people often celebrate the new moon, particularly Rosh Hashanah, for two days for similar reasons.

The following few verses mention the new moon in relation to the 1st Temple. When David was old and had placed Solomon on his throne, he gathered the Levites and priests together. As one of his last works on this earth, David reiterated the details of their specific services in the House of Adonai [20]. The new moon was not forgotten.

> They are to stand every morning to thank and to praise the LORD, and likewise at evening, and to offer all burnt offerings to the LORD, on the sabbaths, the **new moons** and the fixed festivals in the number set by the ordinance concerning them, continually before the LORD.
> (1 Chronicles 23:30-31 NASB)

David passed this knowledge to his son, Solomon. When the new king was prepared to build the House of God as his father envisioned, he also remembered the new moon festival [21].

> "Behold, I am about to build a house for the name of the LORD my God, dedicating it to Him, to burn fragrant incense before Him and to set out the showbread continually, and to offer burnt offerings morning and evening,

20. 1 Chronicles 23

21. See also 2 Chronicles 8:13

33

on sabbaths and on **new moons** and
on the appointed feasts of the LORD
our God, this being required forever
in Israel. (2 Chronicles 2:4 NASB)

Sadly, after the reign of King Solomon, the kingdom
was divided between the north and the south. All
of the northern kings were wicked and only a few
righteous kings ruled in the south in Jerusalem. Out of
Judah's few righteous kings, only one is mentioned
to have remembered the new moon. That king was
Hezekiah.

> And Hezekiah appointed the divisions
> of the priests and the Levites by
> their divisions, each according to
> his service, both the priests and the
> Levites, for burnt offerings and for
> peace offerings, to minister and to
> give thanks and to praise in the gates
> of the camp of the LORD. He also
> appointed the king's portion of his
> goods for the burnt offerings, namely,
> for the morning and evening burnt
> offerings, and the burnt offerings for
> the sabbaths and for the **new moons**
> and for the fixed festivals, as it is
> written in the law of the LORD.
> (2 Chronicles 31:2-3)

Later in the stories of the prophets, the new moon
is mentioned in a very interesting story about the
prophet Elisha and a "great" Shunammite woman.
(2 Kings 4) This barren woman was from Shunem, a
place name that means double blessing. Like the
righteous woman in the Book of Proverbs, she would
call to Elisha anytime he passed through her town
to come in and eat her bread. She even convinced
her husband to make an *aliyah* (lofty, high chamber)
just so Elisha would have a place to rest when he was
in her city.

Her reverence of Elisha's station and her thoughtfulness did not go unnoticed. Elisha asked his servant Gehazi what they could do to repay her kindness. Gehazi mentioned her old husband and their lack of a child. The woman was brought before them, and Elisha prophesied that she (like Sarah) would have a son at that very season (moed) next year; and she does. Sadly, when the child is older and working the fields with his father, a severe headache overtakes him. He is brought to his mother and later dies on her lap. The woman makes haste to find Elisha. As she is leaving, her husband asks her a seemingly strange question:

> He asked, 'Why are you going to him today? It isn't **Rosh-Hodesh** and it isn't Shabbat.' She said, 'It's all right.'
> (2 Kings 4:23 CJB)

For the Shunammite's husband to point out that it wasn't a new moon or a Sabbath, it only makes sense that her custom was to seek the man of God (Elisha) at these festivals. In other words, these were times she set apart to seek wisdom and guidance from YHWH. There are awesome tidbits to be gleaned from the rest of this story. Continue reading in 2 Kings chapters 4 and 8 to locate further associations with the calendar, the moon, the Holy Spirit, and double blessings.

The Book of Nehemiah chronicles the return of the Jewish exiles from Babylon. After Ezra reads the Torah to the people, they repent and agree to RENEW their covenant with Adonai. When the obligations of the Torah are mentioned in chapter 10, the new moon and its offerings are reinstated:

> We also placed ourselves under obligation to contribute yearly one third of a shekel for the service of the house of our God: for the showbread, for the continual grain offering, for

the continual burnt offering, the sabbaths, **the new moon**, for the appointed times, for the holy things and for the sin offerings to make atonement for Israel, and all the work of the house of our God. (Nehemiah 10:32-33 NASB)

The prophet Isaiah has more to say about the new moon than any other Biblical writer, including Moses. His book of prophecy actually begins with a treatise against the House of Judah (southern kingdom). Wicked kings and the surrounding cultures had deeply influenced the way that the people worshiped Adonai. The hearts of the people had grown apathetic and rebellious. They had forgotten YHWH. Thus, their festivals had become vile to Adonai.

When you come to appear before Me, who requires of you this trampling of My courts? Bring your worthless offerings no longer, incense is an abomination to Me. **New moon** and sabbath, the calling of assemblies— I cannot endure iniquity and the solemn assembly. **I hate your new moon festivals and your appointed feasts**, they have become a burden to Me; I am weary of bearing them. (Isaiah 1:12-14 NASB)

This passage from Isaiah (also repeated in Amos 5:21) is often misinterpreted to suggest that Adonai despises His own appointed times. Yet, Isaiah makes it clear to whom he speaking. It was the rulers of Sodom and the people of Gomorrah (see v. 10), not the obedient people of the covenant! Adonai purposefully contrasts His feasts with *your* feasts. His moedim bring freedom, light, and love to the assembly. The works of man brings bondage, darkness, and fear to the Body. Thus, He says, "I hate *your* new moon festivals and *your* appointed feasts, they have become a burden to Me; I am weary of bearing them." Abba loves what He has created and commanded [22]. He hates it when people call evil good and good evil. He hates it when we serve Him for selfish gain. He hates it when we do not tend to the orphan, widow, and poor [23].

Isaiah does give a glimmer of hope for the end. In the last chapter of the Book of Isaiah, he speaks about the final judgment and complete restoration. Below, notice the reversal in the attitudes concerning YHWH's moedim and new moons. All flesh will one day worship Adonai in truth and in peace at His appointed times. No more will the holy moedim (feasts) be kept for dishonest or corrupt reasons, with a hard heart, with malice, or in wickedness. In fact, one day every tongue will confess that Yeshua is Lord [24].

> 'And it shall come to pass that from one New Moon to another, and from one Sabbath to another, all flesh shall come to worship before Me,' says the LORD." (Isaiah 66:23 NKJV)

The prophet Ezekiel also has interesting prophecies about the new moon and the Heavenly (3rd) Temple.

> Thus says the Lord GOD, 'The gate of the inner court facing east shall be shut the six working days; but it shall be opened on the sabbath day and opened on the day of the **new moon**. The prince shall enter by way of the porch of the gate from outside and stand by the post of the gate. Then the priests shall provide his burnt offering and his peace offerings, and he shall worship at the threshold of the gate and then go out; but the gate shall not be shut until the evening. **The**

22. In Leviticus

23, YHWH calls the moedim (feasts) "His" festivals. Above in Isaiah, He calls the moedim "your" feasts. Obviously, the people were keeping the appointed times and new moons for the WRONG reasons.
23 Isaiah 5:20, Deuteronomy 10:18; 14:29, Malachi 3:5, James 1:27

24. Philippians 2:9-11

people of the land shall also worship at the doorway of that gate before the LORD on the sabbaths and on the new moons. The burnt offering which the prince shall offer to the LORD on the sabbath day shall be six lambs without blemish and a ram without blemish; and the grain offering shall be an ephah with the ram, and the grain offering with the lambs as much as he is able to give, and a hin of oil with an ephah. **On the day of the new moon** he shall offer a young bull without blemish, also six lambs and a ram, which shall be without blemish. And he shall provide a grain offering, an ephah with the bull and an ephah with the ram, and with the lambs as much as he is able, and a hin of oil with an ephah.' (Ezekiel 46:1-7 NASB)

Whether the Temple that Ezekiel speaks of is a literal 3rd Temple, a heavenly one that comes down to earth, or both, God's people WILL worship Him on His holy Sabbaths and New Moons.

Hosea was a prophet to both wayward houses of Israel. He relays some very poignant words from the Almighty and one obscure mention about the new moon or month:

> They have dealt treacherously against the LORD, for they have borne illegitimate children. Now **the new moon will devour them** with their land. (Hosea 5:7 NASB)

How can the new moon devour a people? The language is figurative here and can be translated more than one way. Remember, *chodesh* means both month and new moon. Jewish sages and scholars believe that Hosea is referring to a particular month in this passage. The Hebrew month of Av (the fifth month) has seen many tragedies and judgments befall the Jewish people, including the destruction of both the first and second Temples. Truly, if we are walking against the will of Adonai, contrary to the things He allows, the forewarned consequences of doing so can and will bring about events that are dreadful. These things, thankfully, are meant to goad and turn us back toward Him. Read more about the month of Av in chapter five.

Amos also was called to write to God's rebellious people. They abhorred the Sabbaths, festivals, and new moons because it prevented them from profiting from the weak and needy. Their focus was on financial gain and merchandising. Their real love was for self and money, not Adonai and His people.

> Hear this, you who trample the needy, to do away with the humble of the land, saying, **"When will the new moon be over**, so that we may sell grain, and the sabbath, that we may open the wheat market, to make the bushel smaller and the shekel bigger, and to cheat with dishonest scales, so as to buy the helpless for money and the needy for a pair of sandals, and that we may sell the refuse of the wheat?" (Amos 8:4-6 NASB)

The passage in Amos evokes the account of Yeshua overturning the moneychanger's tables in Matthew 21:12-13. Every generation has the potential to turn God's original intent for His House and His festivals into a "den of thieves." But as Yeshua said, "It is written, 'MY HOUSE SHALL BE CALLED A HOUSE OF PRAYER'..." May we never forget His words!

Believe it or not, aside from the quoted Psalms, these are the only references to the new moon in the Tanakh (Old Testament). While the Hebrew word chodesh can be found in other places, the context is clearly referring to a general month and not the new moon festival. However, there is one last reference made in the *Brit Chadashah* (New Testament).

New Moon in the New Testament

The following verses are often used to argue that we no longer need to celebrate the Creator's festivals or calendar. However, if one reads the entire passage in context, Paul is actually saying the opposite. Like him, believers should earnestly desire to meet YHWH at His appointed times because they ARE all about the Messiah [25]! You can explore this notion in another BEKY Book entitled *Colossal Controversies* by Dr. Robin Gould.

> Let no man therefore judge you in meat, or in drink, or in respect of an holyday, or of the **new moon**, or of the sabbath days: which are a shadow of things to come; but the body is of Christ. (Colossians 2:16-17 KJV)

There are limited instances where the new moon surfaces in the written Word of God. Perhaps it is not a coincidence that the moon seems to be *concealed* in the scriptures only to be *revealed* with a few luminous appearances. When we look up into the night sky to observe the *lesser light*, it is apparent that Paul was right. The moon does indeed have its "own glory" [26]. Unlike the sun and stars, the moon's light (from our perspective) is constantly changing. Sometimes its light and glory appears to be fading. Sometimes it is bright and full enough to illuminate even the darkest field. At other times, it has no light at all, and the land appears as dark as pitch.

25. Acts 20:16; 1 Corinthians 11:1

26. 1 Corinthians 15:41

One thing is certain: the verses that DO reference the new moon are usually adjoined to the weekly Sabbaths and the moedim (feast days). The Jewish Encyclopedia states that in pre-exilic times (prior to the Jewish exile in Babylon) that the new moon was celebrated by a cessation of labor that was even superior to the weekly Sabbath [27].

These facts should give readers of Scripture pause and elevate assessment of this festival. Rosh Chodesh was important to the inspired Biblical writers, and is still critical to understanding YHWH's calendar today. Rosh Chodesh, however, is either forgotten or underappreciated by God's people to this day. We can change this. May Adonai enlighten our understanding of the New Moon!

New Moon in Jewish History and Tradition

> Praise Him, sun and moon; praise Him,
> all stars of light! (Psalm 148:3 NASB)

While the new moon is the key to establishing the months of the Biblical calendar, this booklet is strictly about **celebrating the festival** of the new moon, not proper calendar calculating. Nevertheless, it is impossible to completely unravel the calendar from the topic. In light of this, a brief history of the new moon and the sanctification of new months is given with an emphasis on how it is celebrated and announced.

In the time of the Tabernacle and the Temple, the New Moon was celebrated by special sacrifices and by blowing trumpets [28]. The High Priest originally proclaimed and sanctified the New Moon and biblical months since there were specific offerings made. Later, the president of the Sanhedrin took on this responsibility. On the 30th of each month, they assembled in the courtyard of Jerusalem awaiting the reports of new moon sightings by reliable witnesses. Once confirmed,

> ...the president of the Sanhedrin... called out: 'The New Moon is consecrated'; then the whole

27. http://www. jewish encyclopedia. com/articles/ 11493-new-moon retrived February 21, 2016.

28. Numbers 28: 11-15; 2 Chronicles 2:4, 8:13; Ezra 3:5; Nehemiah 10:33

assembly of people twice repeated the words: 'It is consecrated' [29].

Messengers were sent to various cities to announce the new month, but for those regions closer to Jerusalem, signal fires were lit, starting on the Mount of Olives and then from mountain to mountain to spread the news throughout the kingdom [30]. Because word traveled slowly and messengers couldn't always reach their destinations, the proper timing for new months and the effect it had on proper feast day observance was an issue in ancient times. Reading through the history of the Jewish calendar reveals that calendar controversies are far from being a new phenomenon. If communities did not receive the news that the month had begun, how could they celebrate the moedim at their proper time?

The first solution was to have distant communities celebrate Rosh Chodesh for two days. The new moon can appear either 29 or 30 days after the beginning of the previous month. If these areas simply observed the new moon for two days, they would stay in closer synchronization with Jerusalem. This dilemma and the later diaspora eventually led the Jewish governing body to fix the calendar.

Having the people celebrate the holy festivals of God in unity took precedence over exact timing or dating. It turns out that the wisdom of this body ensured Jewish solidarity in the centuries that followed. Being exiled around the globe, a fixed calendar helped the Jewish people to maintain their culture, faith, and identity in foreign lands.

Today, the proclamation of the New Moon has been retained in the liturgy of the Jewish synagogue. On the Sabbath preceding the new month, a special blessing is recited from the *siddur* (prayer book) for the new month. The *chazzan* (cantor) stands at the *bimah* (a raised area) with the Torah scroll, and

29. Mishnah, Rosh Hoshanah 3:1
See also http://www.jewishencyclopedia.com/articles/11493-new-moon retrived February 21, 2016.

30 .Moody, Valerie. *The Feasts of Adonai: Why Christians Should Look at the Biblical Feasts*. Lubbock, TX: Gibbora Productions, 2009. Print. Page 10

the congregation stands to recite the blessing. The chazzan announces the *molad* or the precise timing of the new moon over Jerusalem. This blessing is intended to commemorate the day and to inform the people of the timing of the new month so they may keep track of God's calendar. You can see examples of these blessings in Chapter Six or in a Jewish siddur.

CHAPTER THREE REVIEW

1. What is the difference between the Biblical calendar and the western Gregorian calendar?

2. What does "chodesh" mean?

3. Why do you think that God's yearly calendar begins in the spring with the month in which Passover is celebrated?

4. Explain why Adonai "hated" the new moon festivals and the appointed feast days in Isaiah 1:12-14.

5. Read Colossians Chapters 1-2. What is Paul emphasizing in 1:15-23? Who is the head? Who is the body?

6. Why do you think that Paul draws our attention back to the beginning in 1:15-18?

7. Paul gives a rather long discourse from chapter one to the beginning of chapter two. His purpose was to keep the Colossians from becoming deluded by persuasive arguments (2:4). What sort of things does 2:8 say might deceive them?

8. Could these philosophies, traditions of men, and elementary principles of the world be equated with God's feast days, Sabbaths, new moons, or any other commandment found in the His Holy Word? Why or why not?

9. When we were dead in the uncircumcision of our flesh and in our transgressions, what were the decrees that were against us? (2:14) Was it God's Law or the record of our sins/deeds? (Compare Rev. 20:12) What then, do you think was nailed to cross?

10. According to 2:18, what were the Colossians known to worship? Why was this a problem?

11. Starting in 2:20, Paul describes some of the issues that plagued the people at Colossae. Can the "rudiments of the world" be referring to God's laws, feasts, Sabbaths, or new moons? Let verse 22 inform your answer.

12. Write out Romans 7:14. What is spiritual? What is physical or carnal?

13. According to the above verse, is it possible to associate YHWH's Torah or Law with elementary or rudimentary things of the physical world? Why or why not?

4

HOW TO CELEBRATE ROSH CHODESH

Since there is no working Temple, Levitical priesthood, or a current Sanhedrin ruling in Jerusalem, observing the new moon requires some creativity. While we certainly do not want to add or subtract from the holiness of the day, we can still commemorate it with reverence and joy.

There are many individuals and groups that have made a ministry out of sighting the new moon and creating their own versions of a "correct" biblical calendar. My family chooses to follow the last governing authority from Jerusalem, which aligns us with the current Jewish calendar. You must make your own prayerful decision when it comes to following God's new moons and other festivals, for there are many who claim to have the "right" version.

Whatever you decide, exercise mercy and sacrificial love toward those who choose differently. Without love and respect, observance begins to reek with the vileness spoken of in the passages from Isaiah, Hosea, and Amos. In other words, the focus is on our flesh and self-righteousness, not on YHWH and loving His people.

That being said, there are numerous ways to mark, remember, and celebrate YHWH's new moons. This chapter offers some suggestions for individuals and families, congregations, and even for a women's group. After these recommendations, there is a section listing the Hebrew months along with some traditional themes that you may choose to incorporate into your discussions and celebrations.

Families or Individuals

There will always be months where it is more difficult to organize or attend a meeting specifically for the new moon. However, anyone can at least take a few moments to pause and thank YHWH for bringing him or her into a new month. We can also step outside and look up into the night sky. Children love to look at the heavenly hosts by nature. With just a little effort, a special meal can be prepared. Blowing a trumpet or shofar is another Biblical way to set the new moon day apart as holy. Here is a summary; tailor it to best suit you and your family's personal needs:

1. If possible, prepare a special meal for the family.
2. Near sunset, take your family outside and try to spot (witness) the new moon sliver. This isn't a precise science. Weather can disrupt viewing, or the calendar might be a day off. Just do your best to honor our Creator.
3. Bless the King of the Universe. The *b'rachah* (blessing) for the new month is called *Birkat HaChodesh,* and the blessing specifically for going outside to sight or witness the moon is called *Kiddush Levanah.* These blessings can be found in a Jewish siddur (prayer book) or in Chapter Six of this book.
4. Blow the shofar or trumpet.
5. Offer freewill prayers and offerings.

Congregations or Assemblies

There are a couple of ways that an assembly can recognize the new moon or month. The first is to announce its coming arrival on the Sabbath prior to the new moon. If your assembly is not acknowledging the new month as a body, perhaps you can suggest this to the shepherd and elders. An assembly can easily follow the model that has been preserved by the traditions in Judaism. This form will not take very long and shouldn't interfere with the congregation's normal Sabbath order. There is a sample from the siddur (prayer book) in Chapter Six.

The second way an assembly can recognize the new moon is to establish a meeting especially for this festival. This type of celebration is much more involved and will require more preparation. The examples from both the **Families and Individuals** and the **Women's Groups** can be modified to include more people of both genders and various ages. Again, seek the approval of your shepherd and elders before initiating and opening this type of celebration so that it doesn't become a rock of offense to those we love and respect.

Women's Groups

Since women's bodies follow a natural lunar cycle (menses), the ancient Sages concluded that women are uniquely associated with the varied phases of the moon. Because of this, the new moon in Judaism is considered a woman's festival or Sabbath. Many ladies take this special day to rest from regular work and to gather with other women in worship, song, celebration, and fellowship.

Last year, we started a women's new moon group in my city for this purpose. It has been such an immense blessing to all who attend. Something special happens when the daughters of the Most High come together to honor Him at the new month. We are an eclectic group with various ages, ethnicities, and observance levels, but what we have in common is the King! Our desire is to serve Him at His appointed time.

We typically gather in a home of one of the group members. Here are some of the things that we do (or have on the agenda to experiment with).

1. Blessings

We bless the King of the Universe for the day and an opportunity to gather. We bless the Creator for the moon and its faithful time keeping. We bless Adonai for our wine and bread. (New moon blessings are in Chapter Six.)

2. Candle Lighting

Each lady has a candle, votive, or tea light to represent her light in the world. We light one servant candle (representing Yeshua) and make a blessing to set apart the day. The servant candle is used to light the first lady's candle, and she then lights the woman next to her and so on. The idea is to mimic the signal fires that were once lit from mountain to mountain to announce to the people that the new month had begun. It also signifies how the light of Yeshua in each one of us is used to ignite God's Light in others.

3. Food and Fellowship

We bring snacks, salads, wine, sweet treats, and the like to share a meal. Often the food is themed around the harvests or feasts of that particular month.

4. New Month Discussion

We discuss any upcoming festivals, fasts, or remembrances of the new month. This time could also be used to plan that month's celebrations for families or groups.

We also discuss the Hebrew name of the month and its relationship to God's calendar. A common theme always emerges from the input of each woman. This is rather fascinating to me. The Holy Spirit truly speaks today!

5. Teaching

Often there is a short teaching or deeper explanation of the discussion above. If this is a women's group, teaching could also include the particulars of family purity or other issues that pertain to the women in your group. Prayer, devotions, encouragement, and the like should all be considered.

> Older women likewise are to be reverent in their behavior, not malicious gossips nor enslaved to much wine, teaching what is good, so that they may encourage the young women to love their husbands, to love their children, to be sensible, pure, workers at home, kind, being subject to their own husbands, so that the word of God will not be dishonored. (Titus 2:3-5 NASB)

6. Activity/Worship/Song/Dance

We also use this time to learn from one another. For example, many ladies had never blown a shofar when we first started meeting. Our new moon gatherings gave them an opportunity to learn! These were times of laughter and joy. If you've ever heard the voice of the shofar in the hands of an inexperienced blower, you know that instead of a beautiful melody, it sounds more like a dying cow. We were doubled over in laughter much of the time.

Other ideas are bread making, Davidic dancing,

special music/worship, feast day preparation, making crafts for feast day gatherings, banner or flag making, etc. Recently, we have begun to discuss ways that we can contribute to the less fortunate in our area. Several ladies are gifted with organization and charity work, which gives the rest of us an opportunity to serve where there is a need. We want the marginalized people within our gates to know that there is a Creator and that He loves them!

7. Witness the Moon

We like to physically go outside and look for the new moon. We will often say more blessings and blow the shofar at this time. If the weather is decent, we like to remove our shoes and let our feet touch the earth. There is something special about connecting with our Father's creation in this way as we praise Him for the opportunity to worship Him for another month.

8. Closing Prayer

In these prayers we say whatever is on our hearts. Each woman has an opportunity to speak to Adonai and into the lives of her sisters. This is my favorite part of the celebration!

This is a loose model. The idea is to honor Adonai, fellowship with like-minded women and girls, recognize the new moon, and enter into all of this with joy! You could easily tailor this format to accommodate youth groups, young adults, or even a group of families. Having a plan with structure is a great way to keep everyone's focus where it should be: on Adonai.

5

THE HEBREW MONTHS AND THEIR THEMES

This section lists each Hebrew month, its themes, and other helpful information. It is meant to inspire you to celebrate! Every month there is an opportunity to bless the King of the Universe and to teach children His Ways. **Like the weekly Sabbath, preparation is the key to celebrating Rosh Chodesh.** Once you have determined to observe this festival and have made the proper arrangements for a nice meal or gathering, you might be left wondering, what more can I do?

There isn't a year's worth of Bible verses that deal directly with the new moon; however, the Jewish people have preserved a treasure trove of wisdom about the months. Their traditions and suggestions never fail to reveal a greater depth of knowledge and intimacy through God's festivals. In this case, their understanding in the Hebrew months helps to make connections in the Word that otherwise can be missed. I hope you find it as useful as I have.

This section provides a framework for each month that you can later flesh out with study. Every year these months cycle again. Every month, YHWH has something particular to teach about His and our nature. Every new moon is an opportunity to serve YHWH with the unique theme for that month. This increases understanding and memory.

Under each month heading, you will see these points:

Month
Tribe
Mazel
Middot
Feasts
Themes
Scriptures
Foods

Below these ideas are a few paragraphs under each month that tie the themes together. Use these samples as a springboard for further studies, devotions, or teachings. The month, feasts, themes, scriptures, and foods in the above list are easily understood. The name of each month has a meaning; most months have a Feast Day of YHWH or one from Jewish tradition; and all of these can be associated with various foods to help recall these things. The tribe, *mazel*, and *middot*, however, need further explanation. These concepts were drawn from both the Bible and tradition.

Tribe

The Jewish sages associated each Hebrew month with one of the twelve tribes of Israel. These assignments weren't random. Great thought, prayer, and effort went into this endeavor. They considered the blessings that Jacob and Moses bestowed upon each son/tribe, the Hebrew meaning of that son's/tribe's name, the placement of the tribe's encampments around the Tabernacle, and other factors to make these associations. They are very helpful as a type of devotion or meditation for the month. Feel free to use them or not.

Mazel

A mazel is one constellation in the Mazzaroth (zodiac) [31]. This is NOT to be confused with common New Age astrology. The enemy did not create the heavens with their stars and constellations, YHWH did. He set their courses, and He determines their purpose. The heavens proclaim the Gospel. They do not predict fortunes or one's love life, which is a perversion. Instead, the stars faithfully display the same message year after year, century after century. They are obedient servants of the Most High.

Discussing the month's constellation along with the New Moon is redeeming [32]. The enemy may pervert Godly symbols and heavenly signs like the constellations or the rainbow, but look to their Author, not the deception. Again, please use your own prayerful discretion.

Middot

Middot (middah, singular) are character traits. The Word of God instructs in righteousness. It teaches how a man or woman made in the image of God is supposed to behave. When one learns the difference between the holy and the profane, what is righteous and what is wicked, she can make a decision on how she wants to live. Hopefully, all will choose to walk and live as Master Yeshua did.

A huge part of the Bible is devoted to helping us to "act" right. The Word is concerned with our deeds, not our creeds. This is why "faith without works is dead." Human beings act out what they really believe. When Moses asked YHWH to show him His glory, God revealed thirteen attributes or character traits to Moses [33]. Obviously, if a disciple wants to be the hands and feet of Adonai on the earth, he must show the world this "glory." There are many Biblical

31. Job 38: 31-33

32. Would you like to have a free planetarium right on your computer? Check out http://stellarium.org

33. Exodus 33:18-34:9

55

middot you can learn about and practice, but for our purposes, I have chosen those that correspond best with the festivals and themes for each month.

Middot analysis and practice is usually a part of *Mussar* work. Mussar means correction in Hebrew and is often dubbed "Jewish Ethics" in modern Judaism. Basically, it is focusing on Godly behaviors such as honor, trustfulness, humility, truth, modesty, reverence, faithfulness, forgiveness, honesty, zeal, kindness, etc. By deliberately weighing actions and conduct with these characteristics, it forces one to reflect on his or her inward spiritual life. If one is honest in self-examination and with Adonai, real growth and change can and will happen in the heart. In this way, Mussar becomes a type of soul curriculum that helps us correct weaknesses and improve strengths.

Mazzaroth (Zodiac) in a 6th-century synagogue at Beit Alpha, Israel (Public Domain)

Chodesh Nisan/Aviv

1st Month (March-April)

Month: Nisan or Aviv (Abib), meaning "to be tender or green, miracles, to take flight/exodus"
Tribe: Judah, meaning "to praise YHWH"
Mazel: Taleh (Ram/Lamb) or Aries
Middot: Loving-kindness (chesed), Faithfulness, Loyalty
Feasts: Passover, Unleavened Bread, Firstfruits of Barley
Themes: Redemption, covenant, first love, freedom, miracles, barley harvest, blood of the Lamb, firstfruits, New Year for festival calendar
Scriptures: Genesis 22; Exodus 1-15; Song of Songs 1-8; Matthew 21-28, Revelation 7:9-17
Foods: Matzah, bitter herbs, lamb, barley

> This month [Nisan] shall be the beginning of months for you; it is to be the first month of the year to you. (Exodus 12:2 NASB, brackets mine)

The themes for the month of Aviv (green barley) revolve around the first three spring feasts of Adonai. This is the beginning of months for YHWH's festival calendar, and on a deeper spiritual level, it is the beginning of one's walk and salvation with God. The name Nisan is related to *nes*, miracle. Adonai certainly used many miracles to free Israel and each of us from the bondage of sin and death.

The ram (Aries) or the Lamb redeems from slavery by His blood. Like Judah's namesake, we "praise YHWH" for His mighty hand that creates miracles so that Pharaoh (the enemy) will release us. By the blood, we enter into covenant with Adonai and begin the journey with Him through the wilderness of life. Though the coming months may bring trials or triumphs, we can count on His loyalty and faithfulness even when we fail Him. Our spiritual darkness is pierced by Adonai's spiritual Light.

This chodesh offers the perfect opportunity to focus on *the beginning* in its many aspects. Researching barley in both the Bible and agriculture will bear interesting results that are tied to the themes of Chodesh Aviv. Rereading the stories of the binding of Isaac, the Exodus, and the Passion Week are also helpful.

Chodesh Iyar

2nd Month (April-May)

Month: Iyar or Ziv, meaning "splendor, radiance, and light"
Tribe: Issachar, meaning "to hire or wages"
Mazel: Shor (Bull/Ox) or Taurus
Middot: Patience, Diligence, Adaptability
Feasts: 2nd Passover, Counting the Omer, and Lag B'Omer
Themes: Counting the Omer, transition, being tested in the wilderness, trusting God, second chances, time of healing
Scriptures: Exodus 16; Leviticus 23:15-16; Numbers 9:1-13, 11:31- 35; Deuteronomy 16:9-10; Psalm 105; 2 Peter 2
Foods: Challah bread, quail, coriander

As the second month, division and separation can occur if one does not remain focused on YHWH. *Ziv* means splendor and radiance. Truly, those redeemed on Passover by the blood of the Lamb are a delight to the Creator. Yeshua has paid the **wages** for sin as Issachar's name suggests. Bulls (Taurus) were used for plowing, food, and sacrifice. Yeshua is the strong ox and leader that plows a straight path for His disciples to follow, and it is He who is the true food and sacrifice.

34. Strong's H7794 and H7788 The Hebrew root word for ox is *shur* and means to travel, journey, and even sing [34]. The Pesach

(Passover) meal starts the cycle of the pilgrimage (foot) festivals each year. In chodesh Iyar, the journey or sojourn has already begun. Believers are tallying their steps to the next festival of Pentecost as they count the Omer. Believers can expect to be tested just as the children of Israel were tested before they made it to Mount Sinai. Rereading these accounts sheds light on the spiritual journey.

Tradition teaches that it was in this season that Israel began to lust after meat even though God had provided them with heavenly manna [35]. YHWH's anger was kindled, and as soon as the meat touched their teeth, they died. The people called that place "The Graves of Lust." Sadly, they were only three campsites from Sinai. Thus, during the days of counting the Omer, remember to count blessings and not allow the desires of the flesh to tally its own list of wants. These are days when a believer learns how to discern between God's will and one's own desires.

Issachar is associated with learning and scholarship. This inference is based on the blessing that Moses bestowed upon Zebulun and Issachar. Like them, this month requires a person to draw from the depths of the sea (waters) and thrust his shovel deep into the earth. If he is diligent, he will reap heavenly treasures (wages). Believers must train the flesh to persevere and be patient with others, and one's own limitations. A disciple is to keep putting one foot in front of the other as he or she follows Messiah to the Mountain.

> Of Zebulun he said, "Rejoice, Zebulun, in your going forth, And, Issachar, in your tents. "They will call peoples to the mountain; There they will offer righteous sacrifices; **For they will draw out the abundance of the seas, And the hidden treasures of the sand.**"
> (Deuteronomy 33:18-19 NASB)

35. Numbers 11:31- 35

Chodesh Sivan

3rd Month (May-June)

Month: Sivan, meaning "radiance and covering"
Tribe: Zebulun, meaning "to dwell or dwelling"
Mazel: Teomim (Twins) or Gemini
Middot: Trustworthiness, Responsibility, Awareness
Feasts: Pentecost/Shavuot/Feast of Weeks
Themes: Spiritual freedom, firstfruits, law and grace, giving of the Torah and the Holy Spirit, wedding vows/ketuvah, covenant, Tree of Life, twin loaves of wheat, twin tablets of Commandments, Jacob and Esau
Scriptures: Genesis 25-36; Exodus 19-20; Deuteronomy 16; Ruth 1-4, Matthew 13; Romans 7
Foods: Apples, wine, citron fruits, fish, wheat, honey, and dairy foods. (Milk is considered to be a symbol of the Torah, which nourishes the people just as a mother's milk does for a baby.)

Shavuot (Pentecost) is the central festival on YHWH's calendar. It commemorates both the giving of the Torah and the Holy Spirit. It also features the waving of **two leavened loaves of wheat** in its observance. This is the ONLY time that leaven is allowed in the entire sacrificial system. This is not the leaven of sin and pride; instead, it pictures Israel receiving the pure leaven of the Kingdom of Heaven [36]!

As Zebulun's name suggests, the King desires to **dwell** with His Bride. She must accept His ketuvah (wedding contract), which contains the twins: His Word and His Spirit. The twin loaves could also represent the two tablets of Law, two houses of Israel, Jews and Gentiles, or the Bride and the Bridegroom. However, there is also another aspect that is worth exploring.

36. Matthew 13:31-33

37. Romans 7

Like the Gemini, we each have two natures that war for supremacy [37]. The brothers and **twins**, Jacob and Esau, best depict this other notion. The two opposite natures of these twins represent good and

An Old Cherokee Tale of Two Wolves

One evening an old Cherokee Indian told his grandson about a battle that goes on inside people. He said, 'My son, the battle is between two 'wolves' inside us all. One is Evil. It is anger, envy, jealousy, sorrow, regret, greed, arrogance, self-pity, guilt, resentment, inferiority, lies, false pride, superiority, and ego.

The other is good. It is joy, peace, love, hope, serenity, humility, kindness, benevolence, empathy, generosity, truth, compassion and faith.'

The grandson thought about it for a minute and then asked his grandfather: 'Which wolf wins?'

The old Cherokee simply replied, 'The one you feed.'

Author and True Origin Unknown

evil inclinations. Jacob was a peaceful man that dwelled in tents, but Esau was a cunning hunter, a man of the field.

> And the first came out **red**, all over **like a hairy garment**; and they called his **name Esau**. And after that came his brother out, and **his hand took hold on Esau's heel**; and his name was called **Jacob**: and Isaac was threescore {60} years old when she bare them. And the boys grew: and Esau was a cunning hunter, a man of the field; and Jacob was a plain man, dwelling in tents. (Genesis 25: 25-27 KJV Brackets mine)

The older twin looked very much like a hairy beast when he was born and he is in "the field." Jacob, on the other hand, was a peaceful "man of the tents". YHWH told Rebecca that the older child would serve the younger. If these twins represent the two natures of mankind, then Esau is a picture of the flesh and Jacob is a picture of the spirit.

Man's nature is like a wild, untamed beast that cares for nothing more than its own appetites and desires. Like Jacob, he must learn to master this impulse. The enemy is not always external. The inward war is much more likely to cause harm than an outward force. Shavuot is the perfect time to reflect on our dual natures and the heavenly twosome of Torah and Spirit. God's power twins will ensure that we overcome the sinful nature.

Researching wheat in both the Bible and agriculture will bear interesting results that are tied to the themes of Chodesh Sivan.

> "You shall celebrate the **Feast of Weeks**, that is, the first fruits of the wheat harvest, and the Feast of Ingathering at the turn of the year. "Three times a year all your males are to appear before the Lord GOD, the God of Israel. (Exodus 34:22-23 NASB)

Chodesh Tammuz

4th Month (June-July)

Month: Tammuz, meaning "sprout of life"
Tribe: Reuben, meaning "to see or behold a son"
Mazel: Sarton (Crab) or Cancer
Middot: Truth, Honor, Longsuffering
Feasts: Fast of the 4th Month (17th of Tammuz)
Themes: Overcoming idolatry, the sin of the golden calf, mourning the breach of the Temple walls and its eventual destruction, circumcision of the heart, celebrating Zelophehad's daughters
Scriptures: Deuteronomy 30:6; Jeremiah 4:4; Hosea 14; Ezekiel 8, 36:24-28; Romans 14
Foods: Clean foods [38] with a hard shell that must penetrated or with an outer skin that is discarded

38. Leviticus 11 lists animals that are clean and unclean.

such as eggs, onions, garlic, bananas, citrus fruits, walnuts, pistachios, avocadoes, sunflower seeds, peanuts, or even cheeses encased with inedible wax.

> Thus says the LORD of hosts, **'The fast of the fourth**, the fast of the fifth, the fast of the seventh and the fast of the tenth months will become joy, gladness, and cheerful feasts for the house of Judah; so love truth and peace.' (Zechariah 8:19 NASB)

The month of Tammuz marks the beginning of a long, hot summer before Israel is refreshed again with God's fall festivals. Believers are like little sprouts (Tammuz) that need to mature and grow. This can only happen if one focuses on the Son, as Reuben's name suggests.

Tradition associates Chodesh Tammuz with the sin of the golden calf and Moses breaking the twin tablets. The 17th day of Tammuz is said to be the day that the Romans breached the walls of the Second Temple before its destruction. To remember this tragedy, there is a three-week period of mourning from the 17th of Tammuz until the 9th of Av. Other traditions state that Tammuz was the month that Moses sent the spies out to survey the Land. Their return and evil report is traditionally said to have occurred on the 9th of Av.

The Cancer is a crab, an unclean creature with its skeleton or frame on the outside of its body. In order to reveal the soft flesh of a crab, its hard shell must be penetrated. Hearts are easily calloused to the work of the Word and the Holy Spirit. Hard hearts must be circumcised. One could also associate this with cracking and removing the hard chaff from the kernels of wheat.

Crabs are omnivorous bottom feeders; they feed on

death and refuse, or the things that should be under the feet. Fasting is one sure way to keep flesh in check. During Chodesh Tammuz, it is important that a disciple remain aware of a responsibility to the truth. We must not become distracted by the temptations of the world, which is in reality nothing more than death and decay. When we "see the Son," we cannot allow ourselves to shrink back into our shells or become "crabby" with our neighbors.

> "So circumcise your heart, and stiffen your neck no longer. (Deuteronomy 10:16 NASB)

Chodesh Av

5th Month (July-August)

Month: Av, meaning "Father"
Tribe: Simeon, meaning "to hear or *shema*"
Mazel: Aryeh (Lion) or Leo
Middot: Consolation, Civility/Respect for Others, Empathy
Feasts: Fast of the fifth month (9th of Av/Tisha B'Av), 15th of Av/Tu B'Av
Themes: Mourning and Comfort, hearing and obeying the Father, destruction and renewal, Rachael weeping for her children
Scriptures: Deuteronomy 6, 30; Lamentations 1-5; Psalm 14, 126; Isaiah 52; Jeremiah 31; Zechariah 7:5-10
Foods: Depending on the day(s) of the month, there are times of fasting and times of comforting. Consider comfort foods and other fare that will make a loud crunch such as celery, carrots, tree nuts, or chips. (The latter is to remind us to **hear**).

> "For these things I weep; my eyes run down with water; because far from me is a comforter, One who restores my soul. My children are desolate because the enemy has prevailed." (Lamentations 1:16 NASB)

Av literally means "father." It is customary to add *menachem* to Av, which means "comforter" when speaking about this month. This is because Av is associated with many tragic events, yet the Father brings comfort. Thus, many refer to this month as "Menachem Av" (Comforting Father). Chodesh Av is associated with Simeon (Shimon). Shimon's name means to "hear or shema." In examining the themes associated with the month of Av, it becomes increasingly obvious that our sense of hearing (or lack thereof) is indeed the vehicle by which we will find ourselves either mourning or rejoicing.

> "Say to all the people of the land and to the priests, **'When you fasted and mourned in the fifth and seventh months** these seventy years, was it actually for Me that you fasted? 'When you eat and drink, do you not eat for yourselves and do you not drink for yourselves? 'Are not these the words which the LORD proclaimed by the former prophets, when Jerusalem was inhabited and prosperous along with its cities around it, and the Negev and the foothills were inhabited?'" Then the word of the LORD came to Zechariah saying, "Thus has the LORD of hosts said, **'Dispense true justice and practice kindness and compassion each to his brother; and do not oppress the widow or the orphan, the stranger or the poor; and do not devise evil in your hearts against one another.'** (Zechariah 7:5-10 NASB)

History and tradition records many events when the Children of Israel's "hearing" was tested in the month of Av [39]. Tradition considers the 9th of Av as the date when the ten spies delivered an evil report to Israel and when both Temples were destroyed. History

39. For more on the month of Av, visit: http://graceintorah.net/2015/07/15/month-of-av-tisha-bav-and-tu-bav

records that on the 9th of Av the Jewish people were expelled from Spain (1492), World War I broke out as Germany declared war on Russia (1914), and the deportation began of the Jewish people from the Warsaw Ghetto to Treblinka (1942). Aaron, the High Priest, died on the 1st of Av, another sign of mourning. (Numbers 33:38)

Though the month of Av is connected with judgment and tragedy, it is equally linked to God's mercy. The good news is that even when we are stiff necked or have closed ears, YHWH still loves us. Though the focus of Tisha B'Av is denying oneself and repentance, there should be a transition in the observer that moves the soul from mourning to celebration. We may grieve over past tragedies and rebellions, but our hope is always in the Menachem Av (Comforting Father). It is His divine mercies that give hope for a good future. This is the essence of Tish B'Av. **Remember** the past, but move forward with an attitude of gratitude and a burning hope for a better future.

The Lion or Leo reminds the saints to be overcomers. The Lion of the Tribe of Judah brings the Comforter into our midst, which traditionally begins on the 15th of Av or Tu B'Av. While many destructions and tragedies struck on Tisha B'Av, the 15th ushers in a complete reversal. Instead of ruin, the latter half of the month brings renewal. Some things that traditionally are said to occur on the 15th are the end of the forty year trek through the wilderness, the date that Zelophehad's daughters were granted an inheritance (like sons), and the Benjaminites were readmitted into the community (Judges 19-21).

The book of Lamentations is read on Tish B'Av because it depicts the spiritual and emotional climate of the people after the Kingdom of Judah is overtaken by the Babylonians. Lamentations is called *Megillat Eichah* in Hebrew, which literally means the Scroll of "How!" Jeremiah wonders (as we often do) HOW such calamities can happen to God's people. After reading this mournful prose, one is left feeling empty and hopeless. Where is the Comforter?

Thankfully, the same prophet who wrote Lamentations also wrote the Book of Jeremiah. In Chapter 31, the sorrow of Megillat Eichah is turned into joy with the return of Israel's Comforter.

> **With weeping they will come**, and by supplication I will lead them; I will make them walk by streams of waters, on a straight path in which they will not stumble; for **I am a father to Israel**, and Ephraim is My firstborn." ... Then the virgin will rejoice in the dance, and the young men and the old, together, **for I will turn their mourning into joy and will comfort them and give them joy for their sorrow**. (Jeremiah 31:9, 13 NASB)

The month of Av ebbs and flows with the themes of destruction (judgment) and renewal. Jeremiah, the weeping prophet, captures the spirit of this month like no other. Reading his inspired writings this month is good preparation for the upcoming month of Elul. Though our Adonai is a righteous Judge, He is also the Savior and Restorer!

> As I have watched over them to pluck up, to break down, to overthrow, to destroy and to bring disaster, so I will watch over them to build and to plant, declares the LORD. (Jeremiah 31:28 NASB)

Lastly, remember Rachel and her "weeping" for her children (also mentioned in Jeremiah 31). Why is Rachel weeping? How does this relate to the themes of the month of Av? These are great questions to study and meditate on this month.

Chodesh Elul

6th Month (August-September)

Month: Elul, meaning "nothingness or to search"
Tribe: Gad, meaning "an invading troop"
Mazel: Betulah (Virgin/Woman) or Virgo
Middot: Forgiveness, Decisiveness, Separation
Feasts: Month of Teshuvah, begins 40 days of repentance (ending on Yom Kippur), New Year for Cattle [40]
Themes: Repentance, reconciliation, blowing shofar, mercy, forgiveness, the Bride
Scriptures: Psalm 27; Ezekiel 18; Matthew 4:1-17; Mark 1:14-15; Acts 2:37-41, 17:24-31
Foods: Salt, meat, challah, wine (All are reminders of covenant with Adonai.)

Elul is called "the month of repentance," "the month of mercy," and "the month of forgiveness." It follows the two previous months of Tammuz and Av, traditionally the months of the two great sins of Israel, the sin of the golden calf and the sin of the spies. There are exactly forty days from Elul 1st until Yom HaKippurim (the Day of Atonements) in the yearly feast cycle.

40. Elul 1st is the New Year for the tithing of cattle. The tithe for cattle had to be made from cattle born in the same fiscal year, between Elul 1st one year and the next.

41. Exodus 24:18

Tradition states that Moses' first trip up to Mt. Sinai was on Shavuot (Pentecost) at the giving of the Ten Commandments [41]. Forty days later, he smashed the tablets in response to the sin of the golden calf and then returned up the mountain for an additional forty days to plead for the lives of the Israelites on account of their sin [42]. Moses returned a third time for forty days up the mountain to receive the second set of tablets on the 1st of Elul, returning on the 10th of Tishrei, which is also Yom Kippur [43].

42. Deuteronomy 9:18, 25

43. Exodus 34:28

The four letters of the name **Elul** are an acronym for the initial letters of this phrase in the Song of Songs,"*Ani l'dodi v'dodi li*", which means, "I am to my beloved and my beloved is to me" [44]. This is a common phrase on wedding bands and other religious articles. If we accept Adonai's covenant, we are His Bride. He desires an intimate relationship, one as familiar as a man and wife. When we sin, we are breaking our wedding vows (covenant) with our husband. The penalty should be death, but our Husband is merciful, praise God!

Zilpah bore Gad for her mistress Leah, making him her 5th son. His name means an "invading troop." Leah's words were quite prophetic. She did bear an entire "troop" for Jacob, as she is the mother of eight of the twelve tribes of Israel [45]! The Woman or Virgo is this month's mazel. She is mentioned in the Book of Revelation as having twelve "stars" upon her head.

> A great sign appeared in heaven: a woman clothed with the sun, and the moon under her feet, and **on her head a crown of twelve stars**. (Revelation 12:1 NASB)

In one of Joseph's dreams, Jacob's sons are symbolically represented as stars [46]. Abraham's descendants are also compared to stars in Genesis 15:5. Considering this, who might the twelve stars on the woman's head be in the above verse?

The congregation (Body of Messiah) is also symbolically represented as a woman, bride, virgin, sister, and wife [47]. A wife is like precious rubies and the **crown** of her husband [48].

> **An excellent wife** [eshet chayil] [49] **is the** crown **of her husband...** (Proverbs 12:4b NASB Brackets mine)

Based on these verses and many others, the constellation Betulah mentioned in the Book of Revelation figuratively represents Israel (all of God's people). We are His **troop**, yet we are one. Elul reminds the Bride to prepare for her coming Husband

44. Song of Songs 6:3

45. Along with her maid Zilpah, Leah bore eight of Jacob's twelve sons and his only (mentioned) daughter, Dinah.

46. Genesis 37:9

47. For example: Isaiah 37:22; 54:5-6; 62:5, Jeremiah 2:32; 18:13; 31:4, 21, Lamentations 2:13, Amos 5:2, John 3:29, 2 Corinthians 11:2, Revelation 19:7, etc. Also consider the allegory of the woman in the Song of Songs.

48. Proverbs 31:10

49. Learn more about the Woman of Valor (Eshet Chayil) at: http://graceintorah.net/biblical-role-of-women/

and King. Elul's primary themes are repentance and reconciliation. Israel's desire is to be presented to her Bridegroom as a chaste Bride [50] [51].

Chodesh Tishrei

7th Month (September-October)

Month: Tishrei or Ethanim, meaning "permanence, enduring, ever flowing brooks, to begin"
Tribe: Ephraim, meaning "double fruitfulness"
Mazel: Moznayim (Scales) or Libra
Middot: Righteousness, Reverence/Fear, Justice
Feasts: Rosh Hashanah/Trumpets, Days of Awe, Yom Kippur/Day of Atonements, Sukkot/Tabernacles
Themes: Kingdom, crown, repentance, Book of Life, Book of Deeds, red ones made white, heavenly coverings, God dwelling with us, wedding feast, harvests of wine, oil, and fruits, palm/myrtle/willow branches, sukkah, new Torah cycle
Scripture: Genesis 22; Leviticus 23; Joshua 6:1-21; Judges 4-5; Ecclesiastes 1-12; Psalm 81; Isaiah 27; Joel 2; Matthew 24; John 9:1-7; 1 Corinthians 15; 1 Thessalonians 4:13-18; Revelation 8
Foods: Apples, honey, pomegranates, citron/etrog, round challah loaves, olives, oil, wine, fruit, hearts of palm, dates

50. 2 Corinthians 11:2

51. Learn more about the month of Elul by visiting: http://graceintorah.net/2013/08/07/elul/

52. The four new years are Nisan 1st, Elul 1st, Tishrei 1st, and Shevat 15th.

While Tishrei is the 7th month on the festival calendar, it is the 1st month on the civil calendar, hence, the name Rosh Hashanah or the Head of the Year. Judaism actually celebrates four different New Years [52]. The themes for Tishrei all revolve around the High Holy Days and Sukkot (Feast of Tabernacles/Booths).

The mazel for Tishrei is appropriately the Scales of Justice or Libra. The fall feasts feature the holiest day of the year, the Day of Atonement or Judgment. The King is in the field and He is the only righteous Judge. His Mighty Sword (Word) will divide between soul and spirit and every intention of the hearts of mankind [53]. The Woman or Bride of the Messiah will lay her crown at the feet of the King of kings.

> And when the living creatures give glory and honor and thanks to Him who sits on the throne, to Him who lives forever and ever, the twenty-four elders will fall down before Him who sits on the throne, and will worship Him who lives forever and ever, and will **cast their crowns before the throne**, saying, "Worthy are You, our Lord and our God, to receive glory and honor and power; for You created all things, and because of Your will they existed, and were created." (Revelations 4:9-11 NASB)

Tishrei is an excellent time to focus on the Kingdom of God. If you have children, help them to look up Bible verses and parables that speak about God's throne and Kingdom. Understanding God as the Monarch of the Universe will give you a fresh perspective of the Bible, YHWH, and personal responsibility as His vassals [54].

> "I watched till thrones were put in place, and the Ancient of Days was seated; His garment was white as snow, And the hair of His head was like pure wool. **His throne was a fiery flame**, its wheels a burning fire; A fiery stream issued And came forth from before Him. A thousand thousands ministered to Him; Ten thousand times ten thousand stood before Him. The court was seated, And the **books were opened**. (Daniel 7:9-10 NASB see also Revelation 20:12)

53. Hebrews 4:12

54. For a deeper explanation, read *King, Kingdom, Citizen* by Tyler Dawn Rosenquist.

Interestingly, the rabbis chose Ephraim as the tribe for Chodesh Tishrei. Joseph named his son Ephraim because God had made him fruitful in the land of his affliction.

> He named the second Ephraim, "For," he said, "**God has made me fruitful in the land of my affliction**." (Genesis 41:52 NASB)

The Hebrew word for affliction is *oni* [55]. This is the same Hebrew word used to describe a person's proper actions on Yom Kippur. We are to "afflict" our souls (flesh) on this most holy day [56]. How do we afflict ourselves?

There is a common thread throughout the months thus far. The message from the beginning is the same at the end. Are you a man/woman created in the image of God or a wild beast/serpent of the field? Both were created on day six of creation (the number of man and beast). Both are present in the last book, Revelation. While a beast is not evil in and of itself, a man ruled by these animalistic instincts, lusts, desires, and appetites surely is! Like the twins Jacob and Esau, the older must serve the younger. The beast is older (created before) than the man [57].

We must rule, master, and tame the flesh and conform it to the boundaries of the Master's Word and House. The instructions of God are clear and few compared to the world's endless laws. Our lower nature is free to express its desires within the protective borders of the holy Torah. When a human being steps outside of these guidelines, he or she is no longer in control, and sin is crouching just outside the door (to God's covenant) [58]. This is a lifelong endeavor. It is a daily battle to lay the flesh or beast (nature) on the altar. May we become like Joseph, allowing our afflictions to lead us to a place of double fruitfulness and blessings [59]!

55. Strong's H6040, root anah H6031

56. Leviticus 23:27

57. To learn more about the man and the beast, please see The Creation Gospel series by Dr. Hollisa Alewine; especially workbook four entitled, The Scarlet Harlot and the Crimson Thread. http://thecreationgospel.com

58. Genesis 4:7

Chodesh Cheshvan

8th Month (October-November)

Month: Cheshvan or Bul, meaning "rain, increase, produce, quiet"
Tribe: Manasseh, meaning "cause to forget"
Mazel: Akrav (Scorpion) or Scorpio
Middot: Moderation, Silence, Order
Feasts: None
Themes: The 3rd Temple, Noah's Flood, rainbows, Messiah's Kingdom, serpent on the pole
Scriptures: Genesis 6-8, Jeremiah 31; Ezekiel 40-44; Matthew 2:16-18; Revelation 4:3, 10:1
Foods: Potatoes, beets, and other root vegetables. Try to eat as many colors from the rainbow and Temple descriptions as you can.

The Hebrew name for Scorpio is *Akrav* or Scorpion. Scorpions are unclean creatures that scurry along the ground much like a snake. The word akrav derives from the word *akev*, which means **heel**. Thus the akrav symbolizes the bite of the serpent at the heel of man.

> And I will put enmity Between you [the serpent] and the woman, and between your seed and her seed; He shall bruise you on the head, and **you shall bruise him on the heel**." (Genesis 3:15 NASB brackets and bolding mine)

When the twins Jacob and Esau were born, Jacob's hand was latched onto the **heel** of Esau [60]. The heel is a Hebrew idiom for the lower animalistic (sinful) nature. On the other hand, the head represents the Spirit and Yeshua the Messiah. In a similar vein, the right hand represents spirit, power, and righteousness and the left symbolizes human nature, earth, and worldliness. The tribe associated with Cheshvan is Manasseh. Do you recall what Jacob did when he

59. *The Beast that Crouches at the Door* by Rabbi David Fohrman is excellent resource to explore the dichotomy between the beast and the man.

60. Genesis 25:26

blessed Joseph's two sons?

> Joseph took them both, Ephraim with his right hand toward Israel's left, and Manasseh with his left hand toward Israel's right, and brought them close to him. But **Israel stretched out his right hand and laid it on the head of Ephraim, who was the younger, and his left hand on Manasseh's head**, crossing his hands, **although Manasseh was the firstborn.** (Genesis 48:13-14 NASB)

Jacob or Israel gave the younger son the firstborn's blessing. This upset Joseph and he tried to correct his father, but Jacob insisted. Jacob was also the younger son of his father Isaac, and even though the birthright and blessing belonged to the elder Esau, Jacob received them [61]. The way that Jacob blessed Joseph's sons is another picture of the older serving the younger and a man ruling over his older beastly (sinful) nature. Since the Torah cycle was renewed toward the end of the last month (Tishrei), these stories from Genesis remind us of how to overcome the scorpion or serpent.

The numerical value (gematria) of the Hebrew word Messiah (*Mashiach*) is 358, and the Hebrew word for snake, *nachash* is also 358. Messiah overcame the *nachash* or serpent. As the perfect model, He lived a life in which his flesh never had the upper hand; He was sinless. Reread the story in the wilderness where the people complained and God sent out the fiery serpents to bite them (Numbers 21:4-9). It was their soul or *nephesh* (flesh) that rose up against Moses and YHWH. Understanding that the flesh is akin to the lower (sinful) nature and could be figuratively referred to as a serpent or beast, why do you suppose God sent serpents to bite the people? And why would looking at a bronze symbol of these creatures heal and restore them? Moreover, why do

61. From a worldly or human perspective, Esau as the elder should have received the blessing. Yet, the Bible clearly states that it was YHWH's will that Jacob receive both the birthright and the blessing. In other words, God's Seed isn't always our seed. His ways aren't our ways. In God's economy, the "older (man/flesh) serves the younger (spirit/man)", just as the first Adam serves the second Adam.

you think Yeshua compared His sacrifice and death to this account in Numbers?

> As Moses lifted up the serpent in the wilderness, even so must the Son of Man be lifted up; so that whoever believes will in Him have eternal life. (John 3:14-15)

There are no biblical or traditional feast days during the month of Cheshvan. Tradition teaches that it is "reserved" for the time of Mashiach (Messiah), who will inaugurate the Third Temple during Chodesh Cheshvan. Cheshvan is also called "bul", from the word *mabul* or flood. This is a good time to review the various months mentioned during Noah's flood and the covenant sign of the rainbow.

Chodesh Cheshvan gives a reprieve from the hustle of Tishrei and the time to reflect on how we are going to integrate what we have learned into our daily lives. Hopefully, our prayers and meditations will bring balance to both our spiritual and physical needs.

Chodesh Kislev

9th Month (November- December)

Month: Kislev, meaning "trust, security"
Tribe: Benjamin, meaning "son of the right hand"
Mazel: Keshet (Bow/Archer) Sagittarius
Middot: Gratitude, Compassion, Helpfulness
Feasts: Chanukah (Feast of Dedication/Festival of Lights)
Themes: Dreams, miracles, oil, menorah, cleansing the Temple, overcoming great odds, rededication, Maccabees, Hannah and her 7 sons
Scriptures: Apocryphal Books of 1st and 2nd Maccabees; Exodus 25:31-40; 2 Samuel 22:32-51; Psalm 7, 45, 127; John 10:22-42; Acts 7:55-56
Foods: Foods fried in oil such as latkes (potato

pancakes) and doughnuts, milk, wine, cheesecake

During the month of Kislev, the weekly Torah portions include nine of the ten dreams that are recorded in the Torah (Law of Moses). Because of this phenomenon, Kislev is often called the **month of dreams**. This is interesting on another level: Kislev is the darkest month of the year because it leads up to the winter solstice, but within this dark month, the Festival of Lights (Chanukah) is celebrated. Chanukah is actually a late Sukkot festival. While tradition emphasizes the miracle of oil and the burning menorah, the Book of Maccabees focuses more on cleansing the Temple and rededicating its service to the LORD.

Chanukah means dedication. This dark season is an opportune time to rededicate one's hands to serving YHWH and the Son of His **right hand**, Yeshua the Messiah, as this month's tribal name, Benjamin suggests. The **right hand** of the Archer or Sagittarius is also significant. With it, he wields his mighty bow. He is a great reminder of the power of God's right arm and of the precision with which God works.

> **Your arrows are sharp**; The peoples fall under You; **Your arrows are in the heart of the King's enemies**. Your throne, O God, is forever and ever; A scepter of uprightness is the scepter of Your kingdom. (Psalm 45:5-6 NASB)

The Hebrew word for bow, keshet, comes from the word "to bend." Thus, keshet can refer to a bow and arrows or even the rainbow. Within the Archer are both the covenant and the one that defends the covenant, which is the conquering King Yeshua! A rainbow is a bow that is pointed toward the heavens. If an arrow could be shot through its colorful strings, it would shoot away from earth. This is why the rainbow is a sign of God's covenant and peace. It is His promise to never again destroy the earth with a flood. On the other hand, a bow that points toward the earth would indicate war as the arrows would shoot down to the earth.

> "I establish My covenant with you; and all flesh shall never again be cut off by the water of the flood, neither shall there again be a flood to destroy the earth." God said, "This is the sign of the covenant which I am making between Me and you and every living creature that is with you, for all successive generations; **I set My bow in the cloud, and it shall be for a sign of a covenant between Me and the earth**. (Genesis 9:11-13 NASB)

The Maccabees understood their covenant with Adonai. They wanted to protect and preserve it even though it required them to war against the majority and the invading immoral culture. Their figurative arrows were truth.

The word Torah, often translated as Law, is an **archery** term. It comes from the word *yarah*, which means to cast, throw, or flow [62]. These are the movements an arrow makes as it seeks its target. When human beings sin or break God's law, they are "missing the mark" [63]. The Torah is best translated as "instructions." It is a guide that teaches how to accurately aim arrows to hit the bull's eye. The Hebrew words for teach and teacher share the same root with Torah, *yarah*. A teacher shows how to cast, throw, and flow through life with the least amount of pain, damage, and destruction; they help learners to hit the target. Consider how the prophet Elisha taught King Joash to "shoot" properly:

> When Elisha became sick with the illness of which he was to die, Joash the king of Israel came down to him and wept over him and said, 'My

62. See Strong's Hebrew Numbers H8451 and H3384.

63. The Greek word that is used most frequently for sin is *hamartia*, which means to *miss the mark*. The Torah is the measure of what is right and wrong. As John explained, "*sin is the transgression of the law*" (I John 3:4). All men have "*missed the mark*". An archer's arrow falls to the ground if it is short of its target (Torah). In other words, all have sinned and are in need of a redeeming Savior. We've all missed the mark of the Holy Torah (law). Thus, if a police officer lets you off with a warning (grace) after you've broken a traffic law, that doesn't negate the traffic rule that you broke. It is still illegal to run a stop sign. In like manner, Yeshua's grace does not negate His holy Torah (law).

father, my father, the chariots of Israel and its horsemen!' Elisha said to him, '**Take a bow and arrows**.' So he took a bow and arrows. Then he said to the king of Israel, 'Put your hand on the bow.' And he put his hand on it, **then Elisha laid his hands on the king's hands**. He said, 'Open the window toward the east,' and he opened it. Then Elisha said, 'Shoot!' And he shot. And he said, 'The LORD'S arrow of victory, even the arrow of victory over Aram; for you will defeat the Arameans at Aphek until you have destroyed them.' Then he said, 'Take the arrows,' and he took them. And he said to the king of Israel, '**Strike the ground**,' and he struck it three times and stopped. So the man of God was angry with him and said, 'You should have struck five or six times, then you would have struck Aram until you would have destroyed it. But now you shall strike Aram only three times.' (2 Kings 13:14-19 NASB)

Psalm 127 compares children to gifts, rewards, and **arrows**. There are many more scripture references to bows, arrows, and quivers. Spend some time this month looking them up and pondering their context in both a literal and figurative way.

Chodesh Tevet

10th Month (December- January)

Month: Tevet, meaning "good or tov"
Tribe: Dan, meaning "judge"
Mazel: Gedi (Goat/Kid) or Capricorn
Middot: Righteous Anger, Generosity, Gentleness
Feasts: Last days of Chanukah, Asarah B'Tevet (Fast of the 10th of Tevet)

Themes: Good eye versus evil eye, contrast, judgment, discernment, man and beast, generosity versus stinginess, sacrificial love, overcoming the flesh
Scriptures: Deuteronomy 16:18-20; 1 Kings 12; Proverbs 1, 18; Matthew 6:19-24; Luke 11:33-36; John 7:24; Romans 2; Hebrews 5:12-14
Foods: Simple or bland foods without too many spices.

Tevet has as its root the Hebrew word for good, *tov*. Though this is a winter month when everything appears dead and the air is cold, it reminds a disciple to open his or her hands to those in need. The tribal association with Dan, the judge, indicates that this month requires one to discern between two opposing issues. The battle is typically an inward one. Are we living and acting like a human being created in the image of God, or are we acting more like a selfish beast or snake?

> Dan shall judge his people, as one of the tribes of Israel. Dan shall be a serpent in the way, a horned snake in the path, that bites the horse's heels, so that his rider falls backward. For Your salvation I wait, O LORD. (Genesis 49:16-18 NASB)

> Of Dan he said, '**Dan is a lion's whelp**, that leaps forth from Bashan.' (Deuteronomy 33:22 NASB)

Interestingly, the mazel for this month teaches whom we should follow to gain godly discernment. **The Capricorn is actually a goat with the tail of a fish**. You could say that the goat for Adonai, Yeshua, has the Body of Fish. Yeshua was indeed the most generous man to ever walk the planet. He gave His life for the figurative sheep and for the multitudes of "fish" that compose His Body!

This odd half goat and half fish constellation could

easily be confused with a serpentine-like creature. This is why Dan is the tribal head for Tevet. Dan is compared to both a snake and a lion. Believers must judge between two natures, and maturity level may dictate the choice. The rabbis teach that the test for maturity is in one's ability (or lack thereof) to GIVE.

A person that is generous is said to have a "good eye," and one who is stingy is said to have an "evil eye." These are very common Hebrew idioms. The eye symbolizes our true spirit or nature. Even in English we call eyes "a window to the soul." An immature person is selfish because his sinful nature has the upper hand more often than not. A mature person is generous because the Spirit, the Commandments, and Light always GIVE. Like Dan, believers must learn to judge between these two natures. The differences are often subtle and require a trained eye.

64. The chanukiah is a special menorah used during Chanukah. Instead of the usual seven branches, this menorah has eight branches and one servant branch – *making a total of nine.* The Shamash (servant) candle lights one candle for each of the eight nights of Chanukah **to commemorate the actual seven-branched menorah** that miraculously burned for eight days when the Maccabees cleansed the Temple.

This month begins with the last days of Chanukah when our *chanukiah* [64] is filled with the most light. The chanukiah reminds how the Light of Adonai overcomes the darkness. The 10th of Tevet is a fast day that commemorates the start of the siege against Jerusalem in the year 3336 (425 BCE), which led to the destruction of the first Holy Temple three and a half years later on the 9th of Av. It has become customary during the fast to say a special prayer called *Kaddish* for those whose date and place of death are unknown, such as Holocaust victims.

Chodesh Shevat

11th Month (January- February)

Month: Shevat, meaning "soft branch, rod, or staff"
Tribe: Asher, meaning "happy/happiness, blessed or to walk straight"
Mazel: Deli (pail/water bearer) or Aquarius
Middot: Happiness, Shalom (peace), Modesty
Feasts: Tu B'Shevat (New Year for Trees)
Themes: Trees, new growth, seven species of the

land of Israel, resurrection, Living Waters, fruit, the seed of the woman, River of Life

Scriptures: Genesis 3: 1-8; Exodus 25:31-40; Leviticus 19:23-25; Deuteronomy 8:7-8; Psalm 1; Jeremiah 1:11-12, 2:13, 17:13; Zechariah 14:8; John 7:38; John 15

Foods: Almonds, grapes, figs, pomegranates, olives, dates, wheat, barley, grape juice

Tu B'Shevat or the 15th of Shevat is the day that marks the beginning of the New Year for Trees. This festival originated from the fact that there had to be a division in the year for bringing in the tithes for fruit. Since this is the season that the earliest-blooming trees in the Land of Israel begin to bud, the sages agreed that it would mark the official New Year for fruit tithing.

It is also a time to remember that, "man is a tree of the field" and that Messiah is likened to the Branch [65]. Like trees, disciples have a trunk, limbs, and seeds. They also grow roots and produce fruit, converting *sonlight* into food to produce more branches and fruit. Aaron's rod that budded and the holy menorah were modeled after an almond tree [66]. The Hebrew word for tree, *etz*, is the same word for counsel, **etz**ah. Abraham, Deborah, and King Saul could be found near trees [67]. Moreover, the very first Psalm connects **counsel with trees.**

> How blessed is the man who does not walk in the **counsel** of the wicked, nor stand in the path of sinners, nor sit in the seat of scoffers! But his delight is in the law of the LORD, and in His law he meditates day and night. **He will be like a tree** firmly planted by streams of water, which yields its fruit in its season and its leaf does not wither; and in whatever he does, he prospers. (Psalm 1:1-3 NASB)

Chodesh Shevat is a great time to invite the family to

65. Deuteronomy 20:19; Isaiah 4:2-6; Jeremiah 23:25, 33:15; Zachariah 3:8, 6:12

66. The almond tree is the first tree to bud in the springtime, making it a symbol of wakefulness and resurrection. (Exodus 25:31-40)

67. Genesis 14:13; Judges 4:5; 1 Samuel 14:2

help with some Biblical botany. This is fun for children and adults alike. Research the biblical verses and parables that involve seeds, branches, leaves, and trees. Using a science book or the Internet, follow the life cycle of a tree from seed to fruit. Go outside and collect leaves, seeds, twigs, and the like for children to examine. Then, compare the various parts and functions of trees, people, Torah scrolls, books, and even the menorah [68]. Your findings are sure to be interesting!

The mazel sign for Shevat is the water bearer and is appropriately associated with the New Year for Trees, Living Waters, fruit, happiness, blessings, and Israel. Consider the following verses from the Book of Numbers:

> How fair are your tents, O Jacob, Your dwellings, O Israel! Like valleys that stretch out, like gardens beside the river, like aloes planted by the LORD, **like cedars beside the waters**. **Water will flow from his buckets**, and **his seed will be by many waters**, and his king shall be higher than Agag, and his kingdom shall be exalted. (Numbers 24: 5-7 NASB)

Yeshua, the son of Man, is the water bearer:

> Jesus answered and said to her, 'Everyone who drinks of this water will thirst again; **but whoever drinks of the water that I will give him shall never thirst**; but the water that I will give him will become in him a well of water springing up to eternal life.' (John 4:13-14 NASB)

Those who drink from the Water Bearer's bucket also become a source for the Living Waters as the Book of Numbers mentions above! They will grow up

68. For example, books are made from trees and have heads, tails, spines, backs, joints, and leaves. Torah scrolls also have leaves (pages), crowns, breastplates, hands, and belts. The two wooden spindles that carry the spooled scroll are called "trees of life." The menorah has blossoms, buds, and branches.

69. The prophetess Miriam is also associated with water, find out more here: http://www. graceintorah. net/2014/02/23/ miriams-cup-part-i/

70. *Kreplach* are small dumplings filled with ground meat, mashed potatoes or another filling, usually boiled and served in chicken soup, though they may also be served fried.

strong like the cedar tree [69].

Chodesh Adar

12th Month (February-March)

Month: Adar, meaning "fire, glorious, eminent, high, strength, threshing"
Tribe: Naphtali, meaning "to wrestle"
Mazel: Dagim (fish) or Pisces
Middot: Charity, Temperance, Joy
Feasts: Purim, Fast of Esther (unless it is a leap year) on 13th of Adar
Themes: Overcoming, trading sorrow for joy, giving to the poor, happiness, strength
Scriptures: Esther 1-10
Foods: Wine, fish, vegetables, kreplach [70], sambusak [71], or other foods with filled or hidden centers such as Hamantaschen [72] cookies.

> Then Mordecai recorded these events, and he sent letters to all the Jews who were in all the provinces of King Ahasuerus, both near and far, obliging them to celebrate the fourteenth day of the month **Adar**, and the fifteenth day of the same month, annually, because on those days the Jews rid themselves of their enemies, and it was a month which was turned for them from sorrow into gladness and from mourning into a holiday; that they should make them days of feasting and rejoicing and sending portions of food to one another and gifts to the poor. (Esther 9:20-22 NASB)

The exact meaning of the word Adar is uncertain [73]. However, it is usually associated with strength, happiness, blessings, and rejoicing. Most of the themes and foods associated with Adar are directly

71. *Sambusak* are bite-sized turnovers, like an empanada or a hand pie. They can be filled with cheese, meat, chickpeas, or potatoes. They are either fried or baked.

72. Hamantashen is a triangular filled pastry or cookie that is served on Purim to represent Haman's hat, pockets, or clipped ears (humiliation). Often filled with poppy seeds, various fruit preserves, chocolate, or even cheese. There are various spellings in English for this Yiddish derived word.

73. For example, *Strong's Definitions* states that it is fire, *Brown-Driver-Brigg's Lexicon* defines it as glorious, and *Hitchcock's Dictionary of Bible Names* says it means eminent or high. Adar is also a cognate of the Hebrew word *adir*, which means strength.

related to the Book of Esther and the festival of Purim. However, the consumption of fish is based on the astrological sign of Fish or Dagim.

Fish and other water life were the only creatures not destroyed in Noah's flood [74]. We are like those fish and the Jews of Esther's day. Though judgment or destruction was certain, those who trusted in Adonai were spared. This is something to celebrate! Yeshua compared His followers to fish when He told Peter and Andrew that He would make them "fishers of men." [75] The tribal association of Naphtali, which means "to wrestle or struggle," is reminiscent of the many fish caught in the Master's net. Not one will escape His hand!

> My sheep hear My voice, and I know them, and I know them, and they follow Me; and I give eternal life to them, and they will never perish; and **no one will snatch them out of My hand**. My Father, who has given them to Me, is greater than all; and **no one is able to snatch them out of the Father's hand**. (John 10:27-29 NASB)

Jacob, Naphtali's father, wrestled all night with a "Man" and never walked the same way again.

74. This obviously excludes those that were on the ark.

75. Matthew 4:19; Mark 1:17. See also Jeremiah 16:16 and Ezekiel 47:10

> Then Jacob was left alone; and **a Man wrestled with him** until the breaking of day. Now when He saw that He did not prevail against him, He touched the socket of his hip; and the socket of **Jacob's hip was out of joint as He wrestled with him**. And He said, 'Let Me go, for the day breaks.' But he said, 'I will not let You go unless You bless me!' So He said to him, 'What is your name?' He said, 'Jacob.' And He said, '**Your name shall no longer be called Jacob, but Israel; for you**

have struggled with God and with men, and have prevailed.' Then Jacob asked, saying, 'Tell me Your name, I pray.' And He said, 'Why is it that you ask about My name?' And He blessed him there. So Jacob called the name of the place **Peniel: 'For I have seen God face to face, and my life is preserved.'** (Genesis 32:24-30 NKJV)

Jacob knew that the "man" he wrestled with was God. Interestingly, this is the place where Adonai changes Jacob's name from "the heel catcher" to Israel. Israel means one who wrestles or struggles with God. The Father WANTS His children to wrestle with Him and His Word. **Like Jacob, it is often in the search, struggle, and battle that we meet God face to face.**

Chodesh Adar asks believers to be bold like Queen Esther. She knew the danger of approaching the king unannounced, yet she went forth anyway. It is her famous words that engender courage in the King's servants to this day:

> Go, assemble all the Jews who are found in Susa, and fast for me; do not eat or drink for three days, night or day. I and my maidens also will fast in the same way. **And thus I will go in to the king, which is not according to the law; and if I perish, I perish.** (Esther 4:16 NASB)

Esther teaches another lesson: things aren't always what they seem and hidden things will be revealed. Dig deeply into Esther's story this month. The many fishes of Pisces can learn a lot about the last days, overcoming, and discernment from the Book of Esther [76].

76 Dr. Hollisa Alewine has a fantastic workbook and DVD set devoted to Queen Esther called, *Esther's Mysteries Behind the Mask*. You can find it at www.the creationgospel .com. Another great resource is *The Queen You Thought You Knew* by Rabbi David Fohrman.

Chodesh Adar II

13th Month, Leap Month (February- March)

Please see Chodesh Adar for the themes and meanings of Adar II.

Adar is the 12th and last month of the year unless it is a leap year. When it is a leap year, there is an added month of Adar, making 13 months. This occurs seven times in a nineteen-year cycle and keeps the lunar-based calendar aligned with the solar seasons [77]. In the Fourth Century, Hillel II established a fixed calendar based on mathematical and astronomical calculations. Adar I is added in the 3rd, 6th, 8th, 11th, 14th, 17th and 19th years of the calendar cycle.

When a year has thirteen months, it is called *Shanah Me'uberet*, which literally means **"a pregnant year."** This is a leap year. The additional month is known as Adar I. The extra month is inserted before the regular month of Adar, making the true Adar when Purim is celebrated, Adar II. In other words, Purim is always exactly one month before Passover, whether it is a leap year or not. Sometimes these two months are referred to as Adar A and Adar B.

During leap years, extra themes can be attributed to Adar II. Since the added month makes the year "pregnant," think of double blessings, the mercies of the womb, the concealed being revealed, new growth, and fruitfulness.

Conclusion

Celebrating the new moon in the ways suggested in this book has brought a tremendous amount of joy to my walk with the Creator of heaven and earth. The little group I rejoice with has become knit together in ways that I never expected. We have experienced deliverance, answered prayers, and unity. There is a strong spiritual renewal to push forward and

77. Twelve lunar months make a total of 354 days, which is slightly more than eleven days short of the 365.25-day solar cycle. By adding an additional Adar seven times in a nineteen-year cycle, balance of the seasons and festivals are maintained.

trust in Adonai as we trek through our wildernesses together. Life is hard, but YHWH's mercies are new every morning (and every month). What a blessing to be invited to celebrate with our King! My prayer is that you too will begin to look up at the night sky to examine the moon and anticipate its renewal with delight.

Anyone who blesses the month
in its time is as if he is greeting the
Shekinah (Divine Presence).
-- Talmud - Sanhedrin 42a

6

BLESSINGS AND POEMS FOR THE NEW MOON

The Shehechiyanu

The Shehechiyanu is a blessing that thanks God for sustaining lives so that we are able to experience His appointed times or any other special occasion.

> Blessed are You, Adonai our God, King of the universe, who has kept us alive, and sustained us, and enabled us to reach this season.

Birkat HaChodesh
Blessing the New Month

In the synagogue or in fellowships, on the Sabbath preceding the coming new moon, this prayer is said after the reading of the Haftarah. You may use this blessing at other new moon gatherings if you prefer.

> May it be your will, Adonai our God and God of our forefathers, to renew this month for us with goodness and blessing. Grant unto us long life, a life

of peace, a life of goodness, a life of blessing, a life of sustenance, a life of physical health, a life that reflects a true reverence for God and dread of sin, a life that is free from shame and disgrace, a life of wealth and honor, a life in which we have a love of Torah, Messiah, and an awe of Heaven, a life in which our heartfelt requests are fulfilled for good. Amen.

He Who performed miracles for our forefathers, and redeemed them from slavery to freedom, may He soon redeem us and gather in our dispersed from the four corners of the earth and may all Israel become united in fellowship in the Holy Jerusalem, and let us say, Amen.

The Molad
Time Announcement

If in the synagogue or congregation, the chazzan, pastor, rabbi, or an elder announces the molad or timing for the new moon.

Announce the timing and date of the New Moon:

The new month of _____ will be on the _____ day, which is coming to us and to the whole house of Israel for goodness.

All the people recite:

May the Holy One, blessed be He, renew [name the month] unto us and unto all His people, the house of Israel, for life and for peace, for gladness and for joy, for salvation and consolation, for a good livelihood and sustenance, for good reports, for rains in their season, for complete healing and swift redemption; and let us say, Amen.

Kiddush Levanah
Sanctification of the Moon

The sanctification of the moon is traditionally recited outside when the moon can be seen. It is acceptable to say these blessings up to the fifteenth of the month before the new moon begins to wane.

Psalm 148:1-6

Praise the LORD! Praise the LORD from the heavens; praise Him in the heights! Praise Him, all His angels; praise Him, all His hosts! Praise Him, sun and moon; praise Him, all stars of light! Praise Him, highest heavens, and the waters that are above the heavens! Let them praise the name of the LORD, for He commanded and they were created. He has also established them forever and ever; He has made a decree which will not pass away. (NASB)

One should look at the moon before reciting this following:

Blessed are You, Adonai our God, King of the Universe, Who created the heavens and with the breath of His mouth. He gave them a law and boundaries, that they will not alter. They are master timekeepers for the Most High, joyous and glad to perform the will of their Creator – the

Worker of Truth, Whose work is truth. To the moon He said that it should renew itself as a crown of splendor for those born by Him in the womb, for those who are destined to renew themselves like it, and to glorify their Maker for the name of His glorious kingdom. Blessed are You, Adonai, Who renews the months.

Psalm 121

A Song of Ascents. I will lift up my eyes to the mountains; from where shall my help come? My help comes from the LORD, Who made heaven and earth. He will not allow your foot to slip; He who keeps you will not slumber. Behold, He who keeps Israel will neither slumber nor sleep. The LORD is your keeper; the LORD is your shade on your right hand. The sun will not smite you by day, nor the moon by night. The LORD will protect you from all evil; He will keep your soul. The LORD will guard your going out and your coming in from this time forth and forever. (NASB)

May it be Your will, Adonai, my God and the God of my forefathers, to fill the flaw of the moon that it no longer wanes. May the light of the moon be like the light of the sun and like the light of the seven days of creation [78], as it was before it was diminished, as Your word says: "The two great luminaries." And may there be fulfilled upon us the verse that is written: They shall seek Adonai, their God, and David, their king [79]. Amen.

78. Isaiah 30:26

79. Hosea 3:5

Simple Blessing for the New Moon

A blessing such as the following can be used in a small group or in a women's group. Candle lighting is optional. At our new moon gatherings, each person has his or her own votive or tea light. After saying the blessing, one large candle is lit to serve as the *shamash* (servant) candle. This candle represents the Sanhedrin making the new month official. The shamash candle lights the person closest on the right and that person lights the next one closest to their right and so on. This commemorates the signal fires that were lit from mountain to mountain in ancient times to announce the new moon. It also signifies the light that each believer is given by the Messiah Yeshua. We spread His Light!

> Blessed are You, Adonai, Who gives us the New Moon, the sign of being born from above and continual renewal. Blessed are You, Adonai, Who renews His mercies every morning and gives us countless opportunities to repent and start fresh. May the ancient light of the moon's face never cease from reminding us of Your truth, Your love, and your saving grace.
>
> May the Holy One, blessed be He, renew [name the month] unto us and unto all His people, the house of Israel, for life and for peace, for gladness and for joy, for salvation and consolation, for a good livelihood and sustenance, for good reports and tidings, for rains in their season, for complete healing and swift redemption; and let us say, Amen.
>
> (Light shamash candle, then other candles if using.)

Poems for Rosh Chodesh

Meditating on the waxing and waning of the nightly moon phases, and its silent presentation of the Gospel, can have a cathartic effect on the soul. The following two poems are a result of such reflections. I pray you will allow YHWH's moonbeams to creatively flow through you as well.

The Moon Walks

By Sarah S. Walters
Sewnolivette.com

The moon walks
In faithfulness.
Returning,
Renewing,
Month after month
Back to her place
Of closeness
With the sun.
Each time she obscures
Herself in darkness
From the eyes of the world,
Her hidden nature
Is bathed in the light
Of that radiant star.
Though her way
Appears inconstant
To those who live on earth,
From the viewpoint
Of the shining luminary,
A part of her
Always
Reflects his glory.

Luny Tunes

By Deborah Flanagan

From in the beginning,
The Ancient of Days
Orchestrated the rhythms
to govern all ways
Creation methodically
flows through the score
Our hearts beating tempo
to whispering chords
With budding and birthing,
the ebb and the flow
Of movement, of moment,
of life's crescendo
The composer has set
soundless, shadowed or full
A luminary maestro
of magnetic pull
This keeper of time
has no voice of his own
But fixed is his order,
a grand metronome
Appointed he stands
to meter the time
filling reprise
with rhythm and rhyme
Rising and falling,
the wax and the wane
Broadens the melody's
subtle key change
There's harmony there
for all who have ears
and yearning of spirit
to dance through the years
New moon leads a song
that our Savior composed
And as light's drawing nearer,
the shadow, it grows.

FURTHER READING

Esther's Mysteries Behind the Mask by Dr. Hollisa Alewine

What is the Torah? by Dr. Hollisa Alewine

Celebrating the New Moon: A Rosh Chodesh Anthology by Susan Berrin

The Witness of the Stars by E. W. Bullinger

The Beast That Crouches at the Door: Adam & Eve, Cain & Abel, and Beyond: A Biblical Exploration by Rabbi David Fohrman

The Queen You Thought You Knew: Unmasking Esther's Hidden Story by Rabbi David Fohrman

Colossal Controversies by Dr. Robin Gould

Everyday Holiness: The Jewish Spiritual Path of Mussar by Alan Morinis

The Wisdom in the Hebrew Months by Tsevi Raizman and Yehuda Heimowitz

The Rosh Hodesh Table Foods at the New Moon by Judith Solomon

Mazzaroth, or the Constellations by Frances Rolleston

King, Kingdom, Citizen: His Reign and Our Identity by Tyler Dawn Rosenquist

The Gospel in the Stars by Joseph A. Seiss

REFERENCES

Alewine, H. (2012). *The creation Gospel workbook one: the creation foundation (revised)*. London, KY: The Creation Gospel.

_____ (2012) *The scarlet harlot and the crimson thread*. London, KY: The Creation Gospel.

Benner, J. *Ancient Hebrew research center*. Retrieved 06 Mar. 2016. <http://ancient-hebrew.org/>.

Kholer, K. *New moon*. Retrieved 21 February 2016. http://www.jewishencyclopedia.com/articles/11493-new-moon.

Martin, D. (1996). *That's Amore: the Best of Dean Martin*. Capitol. MP3.

Mishnah Rosh Hashanah 3:1.

Moody, V. (2009). *The feasts of Adonai: why Christians should look at the biblical feasts*. Lubbock, TX: Gibbora Productions.

ABOUT
THE AUTHOR

Kisha Gallagher has been studying the Hebraic roots of Christianity since 2004. She is the author of the website, Grace in Torah, a ministry devoted to the study of the Word, the Gospel of Yeshua, the moedim (feasts) of Israel, marital roles, and living out a Torah lifestyle. She encourages the young and old alike to draw deeply from the wells of salvation (Is.  12:3), for all are welcome. Kisha is a devout student of the Word and a minister of the Good News. Many lives are touched through her website, conference engagements, and weekly small groups. Kisha resides with her loving husband near the Smoky Mountains where she homeschools their children. She enjoys research, canvas painting, writing, teaching, discipleship, and gathering with the Body of Messiah. She also has a passion for women's ministry and considers herself an abolitionist. She supports the fight against human trafficking and enslavement whether it is physical or spiritual. Mrs. Gallagher can be contacted at graceintorah.net.

Made in the USA
Charleston, SC
12 September 2016